D1715307

Published by Cambridge House Press
New York, NY 10001
www.CamHousePress.com

Cover design by Jon Wyble and Jessica Gardner
Composition/typography by Amanda Lehner and Rachel Trusheim

Library of Congress Cataloging-in-Publication Data

Brown, Barrett.
 Flock of dodos : modern creationism, intelligent design & the Easter bunny /
Barrett Brown, Jon P. Alston.
     p. cm.
 ISBN 0-9787213-0-6 (hardcover)
 1. Creationism. 2. Intelligent design (Teleology) I. Alston, Jon P., 1937-
II. Title.

 BS651.B78745 2007
 231.7'652--dc22

                              2006034100

This book is intended as satire. Any viewpoints and opinions expressed in this
book belong to the authors and subjects and are in no way endorsed by Cambridge House Press, its employees, principals or those involved in work-for-
hire. Besides, the Easter Bunny sublets from our Publisher in the off-season.

10 9 8 7 6 5 4 3 2

Printed in the United States of America.

FLOCK OF DODOS

Behind Modern Creationism, Intelligent Design & the Easter Bunny

Barrett Brown
Jon P. Alston, Ph.D.

CAMBRIDGE HOUSE PRESS
NEW YORK § TORONTO

DODO CONTENTS

ONE

In Yahweh We Trust

We are dealing here with something more than a straightforward determination of scientific facts or confirmation of scientific theories. Rather we are dealing with competing worldviews and incompatible metaphysical systems.

– **William Dembski, *Intelligent Design***

Let me make the superstitions of a nation and I care not who makes its laws nor its songs.

– **Mark Twain**

The largest problems are often the easiest to ignore. Just as often, they're also the hardest to fix. This is why the largest problems tend to remain large and problematic forever.

Consider the federal deficit. It's easy to ignore because it's boring, and it's hard to fix because, deep down, no one really gives a damn about it. Of course, members of whichever political party is sidelined at the moment will occasionally express varying degrees of existential angst over the whole thing, and every once in a while a cranky senior citizen will write a strongly-worded letter to his local newspaper in which runaway spending is denounced in no uncertain terms. But the politicians are just doing their jobs, or at least going through the motions of such, and the cranky writer simply has too much time on his hands; next week he'll be denouncing the laxity of leash law enforcement with equal vigor.

Next time you're at a bar, try to start a fight over a national budget shortfall. You'd be hard-pressed to get a rise out of a coked-up Hell's Angel at three in the morning. Mad Dog just doesn't care. Most likely, you don't either. Neither do I, to be perfectly honest. And the nation's political strategists are fully aware that neither you nor I nor Mad Dog himself is likely to give much thought to the deficit when we all go to the polls, and that the only fellows who might actually do so are a couple of editors over at *The Economist* and perhaps Ross Perot. But the editors of *The Economist* can't vote because they're Brits, and Ross Perot is just going to vote for himself anyway.

The political strategists are aware of this as well. So the deficit is here to stay, and for every cover story that *Newsweek* runs on the subject, it will also run at least eight others covering all-natural arthritis treatments. This may be considered to be a law of nature.

But not every large problem facing the nation need be regarded so fatalistically. Some of these large problems are neither easy to ignore nor hard to fix – which means that they not only *can* be solved, but even *might* be solved.

One of those rare, lucky problems is the latest assault on the theory of evolution. It's hard to ignore because it's sexy and far-reaching in its implications, the sort of thing that might compel someone to write a tired cliché on a piece of cardboard and demonstrate in front of a county courthouse. And it's easy to fix because the ones leading the assault are the sort of people who actually do that sort of thing.

Unlike the deficit, the war over evolution is an emotional issue. But like the deficit, it's also an important issue that deserves an honest, straightforward explanation.

If one were to write a book with the intent of explaining the root causes of the current federal deficit, an honest writer would naturally feel compelled to report these causes without regard to any toes he might be stepping on in the process. And despite the subject's relative lack of emotional immediacy, toes would indeed have to be stepped on – congressmen, lobbyists, and pressure groups of every stripe and flavor would have to be cited for their faults, hallowed institutions like the farm subsidy racket would have to be taken apart and examined in a rather unceremonious fashion, and a good portion of the voting public itself would have to be scolded, subjected to severe finger-wagging, and otherwise called to account for allowing such silly things to happen in the first place. This would certainly make some people cranky. In the end, though, the book will have accomplished its purpose of providing the skinny on the deficit.

Similarly, the intent of this book is to explain the current battle over evolution. Like our hypothetical screed concerning the deficit, this book obligates us to step on some toes. But because of evolution's wider implications, we are required to do more than that. By the very act of pointing out certain facts, we not only step on toes, we also cut them off. Now, this is a very painful process to be sure, and one can't help but feel a bit of sympathy for those whose toes will soon go missing. But the process is unavoidable, lest we all lose our heads in the end.

This will not be a polite book. Politeness is wasted on the dishonest, who will always take advantage of any well-intended concession, and the leaders of the so-called "Intelligent Design" movement, as we shall see, are so incredibly dishonest that they could cause a veteran heroin addict to blush – not out of any moral objection on the part of the addict, but rather out of embarrassment that anyone could be so darned bad at lying. And, as we shall see, the Intelligent Design folks are bad liars indeed.

"But why do the Intelligent Design folks lie?" you ask. A very perceptive question, Gentle Reader. Also, you're looking quite dapper today. Have you lost weight? Not that you needed to in the first place. You carry it well.

The answer is that they lie for the same reason that I just did, or that the heroin addict does – they lie because they want something, but they don't want you to know the true nature of what they want. Just now, I lied to make a point on the sly – I have no way of knowing if you really are perceptive, or if you look any more dapper today than you did yesterday, or if anyone still says "dapper" anymore, or whether or not you lost weight or needed to in the first place. For all I know, you could be some sort of half-literate water buffalo. If so, you have my condolences.

Unfortunately, lies intended to prove points are a rare sort indeed. More common are the types of lies told by heroin addicts.

Scenario One: *The Heroin Addict Meets a Good-Natured Sucker*

"Excuse me, but I've just run out of gas down the street. Can you give me, like, five bucks? I'm trying to get some gas. You can tell, because I'm carrying this cheap plastic gas can."

"Hey, you sure are. That's proof enough for me. Here's five."

"Oh, hey, thanks. Uh… could you make it ten? The Republicans are back in power and oil prices are up."

"Sure thing, buddy! Gosh, you know who would like you? My virginal, naïve, seventeen year-old daughter. Hell, let's take you home and set the two of you up right now!"

"Sounds good. But, uh, let's take your car."

Scenario Two: *The Heroin Addict Meets Acclaimed British Scientist Richard Dawkins, With Apologies to Acclaimed British Scientist Richard Dawkins for Stealing His Persona Without His Authorization*

"Excuse me, but I've just run out of gas down the street.

Can you give me, like, five bucks? I'm trying to get some gas. You can tell, because I'm carrying this cheap plastic gas can."

"I do indeed observe that you appear to be carrying a cheap plastic gas can."

"Uh… huh?"

"Where's your car, sir?"

"It's, uh, down the street."

"Let's have a look, shall we?"

"Uh… I'd better go now.

"Perhaps you'd better. By the way, you resemble a water buffalo."

Scenario Three: *The Heroin Addict Meets Yet Another Heroin Addict, Probably in Portland or Somewhere Dreary Like That*

"Excuse me, but I've just run out of gas down the street. Can you give me, like, five bucks? I'm trying to get some gas. You can tell, because I'm carrying this cheap plastic gas can."

"Hey, you must be a heroin addict, too. Let's work together in secret in order to advance our shared goals; namely, shooting up lots and lots of heroin."

"Okay."

"Can we use your car?"

"Uh… I don't have a car."

"Oh, right, I forgot. You're a lying heroin addict, like myself. We'll take my car, then."

"You've got a car?"

"Actually, no. I was lying, too."

"High-five!"

"Right on!"

The Good-Natured Sucker is the American public – generally honest and well-meaning, but not quite wise to the tricks of heroin addicts. Richard Dawkins is a brilliant scientist who's savvy enough about life to know when he's being lied to. And the heroin addicts are the "prime movers," so to speak, behind Intelligent Design – they lie to others when they find it convenient, and speak the truth only to each other. For the sake of clarity, let's call these two hypothetical heroin addicts "William Dembski" and "Michael Behe." Coincidentally enough, William Dembski and Michael Behe are actually real people. This is unfortunate, but true nonetheless.

As two of the leading proponents of Intelligent Design, William Dembski and Michael Behe are not addicted to heroin. They are addicted to the Dark Ages. And they wish you to be addicted to the Dark Ages as well.

Yes, it's cruel to cut off toes. But in addition to being necessary, it can be fun, at least on occasion.

This is one of those occasions.

* * *

In 2004, a retired prison supervisor by the name of William Buckingham was appointed head of the Dover Area School District's board curriculum committee. That same year, the committee was asked to purchase new biology textbooks for those students unfortunate enough to attend school in the sort of place where retired prison supervisors are given authority over cutting-edge educational issues. Over the course of the discussions, disputes arose, a vote was called, and just a year later, Dover found itself immersed in a sort of Scopes Monkey Trial Redux.

Because the Dover incident was such an exceptional event in the greater battle between evolution and creationism, much more will be said on it in a later chapter. But whereas the Dover incident is exceptional enough to be put off until it can be placed in its proper context, William Buckingham is so perfectly unexceptional that any introductory chapter to a book like this would be incomplete without him.

So, then, let us get to know William Buckingham.

The U.S. District Court for the Middle District of Pennsylvania got to know William Buckingham fairly well during the Dover incident. This wasn't an accident, either, as the outcome of *Kitzmiller v. Dover Area School District* would be determined in part based upon what exactly was going through the respective heads of Buckingham and his fellow board members when they voted to include the following statement in the district's biology curriculum:

> "Students will be made aware of the gaps/problems in Darwin's theory and of other theories of evolution including, but not limited to, Intelligent Design. Note: Origins of life is not taught."

In addition to adding the written disclaimer, Buckingham's faction also succeeded in requiring science teachers to read another longer, more awkwardly-worded disclaimer to ninth-grade biology students, in which said students were reminded that "Darwin's Theory" is "not a fact," and that "gaps in the Theory exist for which there is no evidence." To top it off, the anti-Darwin contingent also managed to have a popular Intelligent Design volume called *On Pandas and People* included in the science program as a supplementary reference text. This had been the result of a compromise; Buckingham and his allies had originally sought to replace the textbook recommended by science teachers with another of their own choosing.

When *Kitzmiller* finally went to trial, the strategies were clear – the defense would have to show that Buckingham et al were simply acting out of a concern that students were getting an incomplete picture of controversies in modern biology, while the prosecution would have to demonstrate that they had instead been acting out of a purely religious motivation, thus rendering the end result unconstitutional. As it turns out, the prosecution had the easier job.

Part of the problem for the defense was that Buckingham was incapable of keeping his story straight. Whereas he testified several times during both the trial and his earlier depositions that he had simply been seeking to provide students with a more "balanced" view of evolution, elsewhere he was forced to admit that he had criticized one proposed textbook as being "laced with Darwinism," as if this in itself was a clear negative. He also seemed to have trouble deciding whether or not he himself had been an active part of the effort to push for Intelligent Design; during his cross-examination, Buckingham denied the prosecutor's characterization of himself as "the one who kept the conversation going." The problem here was that the prosecutor's characterization was exactly the same that Buckingham himself had used during his deposition, during which he plainly stated, "I was the board member who kept the conversation going." In another instance, Buckingham admitted to having once told a reporter that "this country wasn't founded on Muslim beliefs or evolution. This country was founded on Christianity, and our students should be taught as such." During his earlier deposition, though, he had denied ever uttering those words. As the cross-examination played out, minor discrepancies such as this popped up regularly.

To be fair, Buckingham could certainly point to a hazy memory regarding some details, having spent part of that time period recovering from an addiction to Oxycontin, a powerful painkiller which he'd been prescribed in response to some ongoing medical issues. As such, he could reasonably claim forgetfulness when it came time to explain away these discrepancies as simple mistakes, and he did indeed claim this privilege several times.

Oddly enough, though, whenever a dispute arose regarding something a bit more sensitive – something that could have painted the witness and his buddies as having acted with a religious intention in a public capacity, for instance – Buckingham suddenly transformed into something of a human stenograph. During his cross-examination, he denied that any board member had openly advocated the teaching of creationism during school board meetings; when faced with nearly a dozen written accounts from two local newspapers in which board members were said to have done so, Buckingham steadfastly denied it, claiming that the reporters involved had simply made up the accounts, quotes and all. No one, Buckingham claimed, had been pushing for creationism in their public capacities, secretly or otherwise.

This didn't quite turn out to be the case. One board member by the name of Heather Gessey had actually written a letter to the editor of a local paper in which she'd asserted that "you can teach creationism without it being Christianity." When confronted with this piece of evidence, Buckingham had little to say beyond, "I don't read her mail."

Fair enough. But then the prosecutor produced another piece of evidence – a clip from the local Fox affiliate in which Buckingham had told a reporter, "It's okay to teach Darwin, but you have to balance it out with something else, like creationism." This time, Buckingham had plenty to say.

"Due to the different atmosphere I was placed in, I think that was the first time I was ever interviewed by anyone since I had been on the school board, and I think it was a combination of fright, the change in the atmosphere, and I was just like I said I felt like I was a deer in the headlights of a car, and I concentrated so hard on not saying creationism, I made a human mistake and I said it," he told the court.

So the prosecutor played the clip again.

"You didn't look very pressured to me," he said. "Is there something in that tape that suggests to you that you were feeling pressured at the time?"

"I can't help how it looks. I'm telling you I felt pressured at the time."

Despite the apparently horrific effect that this brief interview with a dinky local news affiliate seemed to have had on the veteran prison supervisor, Buckingham seemed to have no recollection of it during his earlier deposition, when he was specifically asked whether or not he had ever publicly advocated the teaching of creationism. Perhaps the trauma was so great that he had no choice but to block it out of his mind, lest the sheer animalistic terror he had experienced replay itself over and over again, eventually destroying his psyche and leaving him an empty shell of a man. Or perhaps Buckingham was simply lying his ass off. It's hard to say. But for his part, the prosecutor wasn't content to simply force Buckingham to relive traumatic memories.

"You don't have any background in science, do you, Mr. Buckingham?"

"No, I don't, nothing formal."

"Excuse me?"

"Nothing formal, no, sir."

"And, in fact, the school district has some paid professionals who are knowledgeable in the area of science education, doesn't it?"

"Yes, they do."

"Those are the science teachers, right?"

"That's true."

"So you disregarded or the board disregarded the view of the only scientific education advisors that it had. Isn't that correct?"

"We did not disregard it. We considered it when we made our decisions."

"Mr. Buckingham, you don't even know whether Intelligent Design is considered good science, do you?"

"In my opinion, it is, and in the opinion of a lot of scientists, it is."

"Well, at your deposition, Mr. Rothschild asked you about this, and you said that you didn't even know whether it was good science. Do you remember that?"

As you might expect by this point, Buckingham didn't remember it at all. Nonetheless, it was true. Buckingham had neither seemed to know nor care whether Intelligent Design was "good science." But for some reason, he wanted it taught in public school science classes. How odd! It was almost as if Buckingham had been acting on some other motivation. But if his motivation wasn't scientific in nature, then what could it have been? Gee, what's the opposite of "science?"

The prosecutor seemed to have an inkling. And so he moved on to the subject of the 60 copies of *On Pandas and People* that had been donated to the school under originally mysterious circumstances. By the time of the trial, it had been established that it was Buckingham who had organized the fundraising for this project; in fact, as Buckingham was willing to admit at this point, he himself had appeared before the congregation of his church to ask for donations – although Buckingham wouldn't necessarily characterize it that way.

"And, in fact, you took up a collection at your church for *On Pandas and People*. Right?"

"Not as such I didn't, no."

"Well, you did take up a collection at your church. Right?"

"Money was donated, but I didn't ask for it."

"You stood in front of your church, in the Harmony Grove Community Church, and you made a statement that you were accepting donations for the book *On Pandas and People*. Correct?"

"No, I didn't. I'm sorry, I did say that, but there was more to it."

"In fact, you checked with one of the church elders before getting up to make that statement to see if it was okay if you could make that statement at the front of your church. Correct?"

"I spoke to the church elder to ask if I could have about two minutes prior to the church starting to address the congregation, yes."

"And this was on a Sunday?"

"Yes."

"And you stood not in the pulpit but in the front of the pews while people were actually in the church. Right?"

"Yes."

"And you said that there's a need, we don't want to use taxpayer dollars, and if you feel led to donate, fine. I'm not asking for money, I'm just letting you know that there's a need. That's what you said. Right?"

"That's true."

So Buckingham didn't ask the members of his church for money. He simply informed them that money was needed for something and that they should provide it. Quite a bucket of nuance, that Buckingham. But the prosecutor's strategy here wasn't just to force the hyper-conservative Buckingham into suddenly channeling Bill Clinton; this was simply a buildup to something more significant.

"Mr. Buckingham, do you really think that the people at your church would have given money for this book if they didn't think that there was some religious connection to it?"

"The people in our church give money to a lot of things. This book was one thing of many that they donated money to, and it's not always because of a religious thing."

"Do they usually donate money to public schools, or, better yet, have they ever donated any money to any public school before?"

Buckingham's answer was priceless.

"I don't know. I've only been going to church there for ten years."

But this was just another rung on the ladder for the prosecutor.

"And at a board meeting in the fall of 2004, a question was raised by a man named Larry Snoke, who was a former member of the board, about who donated the copies of *Pandas* to the school district. Right?"

"Yes, I remember that."

"And the board didn't provide any answer to Mr. Snoke's question, did they?"

"I don't recall what the response was."

"Well, you didn't speak up and say that you knew where the money came from, did you?"

"No, I didn't."

"And are you aware that Mr. Alan Bonsell spoke up and said he knew where the money came from?"

"I don't remember him saying that."

"And the reason why you didn't speak up at the board meeting in the fall of 2004 about who donated the money for the donation of *Pandas* is because you didn't want anybody to know that the money was raised at a church. Isn't that true?"

"That's not true. I didn't – I couldn't say who donated the money because I didn't know where the cash came from."

What Buckingham meant here was that he couldn't name the individual donors, with the exception of one who wrote a check, because donations were deposited in cash at a church mailbox.

"So you just knew that it came from members of your church, but you didn't know which specific members of your church. Right?"

"As far as the cash goes, that's true."

"And there was also one check, and you knew who that came from. Right?"

"Yes, I do."

"And you think that because you didn't know the specific names of the people at your church who gave the money, that you shouldn't tell this former board member, this member of the public, where this – that the money for the donation was collected at your church. You didn't think you should share that information. Right?"

"I didn't see where it was relevant."

"Well, actually, you wanted to hide that information. Isn't that true, Mr. Buckingham?"

"No. If someone would have asked me if it came from the church, the people at the church, I would have told them it did, but it never came up."

"Well, Mr. Buckingham—"

"It was put to us, who donated the money, and I don't know who did. I know there were people in a certain setting that did, but I don't know who they were."

"If someone had asked you specifically about that, you would have told them. Right?"

"Asked me about what?"

"About who donated the money."

"I don't know who donated the money."

"I'm asking you, if somebody had asked you specifically who donated the money, you're telling us you would have told them. Right?"

"As far as the cash goes, yes."

"Well, as a matter of fact, Mr. Buckingham, I asked you specifically who donated the money, and you didn't tell me at your deposition on January the 3rd, 2005. Isn't that true?"

Oops!

Here's how that part of the deposition had gone down:

"The school district received a number of copies of the book *Of Pandas and People*. Correct?"

"Yes."

"Do you know how many copies?"

"I've been told there were 60. I haven't seen them."

"Do you know where that came from, who donated the money?"

"No, I don't."

"You have no idea?"

"I have thoughts, but I don't know."

"What are your thoughts?"

"I think it could have a tie to Alan Bonsell, who was board president at the time."

"Why do you think – I know you're not saying it was,

but why do you think it might have ties to Mr. Bonsell?"

"Because he was the president of the board at the time, and I just deduced from that."

Far be it for anyone to question Buckingham's deductive skills, but let us quickly apply our own. If someone organizes a donation drive, then claims to have "deduced" that it was someone else entirely who organized that very same drive, that person is probably lying. But wait, there's more! From the same deposition:

"Were you ever at a board meeting where someone asked who donated the book to the school, in fact, Larry Snoke, a former board member asking who donated it?"

"I think he expressed a wonder-type thing over where they came from. I don't think – I don't remember anybody asking directly where they came from."

At this point in the deposition, the prosecutor seemed to express a "wonder-type thing" over why it was that Buckingham hadn't seen fit to find out who might have spearheaded such a charitable act. Surely a thank-you note would have been in order, at the very least.

"Were you curious to know where the book came from?"

"I know they came from someone in the public sector. I know we didn't use taxpayer funds to pay for them."

"Did you ask where it came from?"

"No."

"Why didn't you ask?"

"Didn't want to know."

"Why didn't you want to know?"

"Well, what purpose would it serve?"

"Well, because you're a board member and the school district is part of your responsibility as a board member and maybe where these books came from would be something that you should know."

"No, I think it was a wonderful gesture, and I didn't

concern myself with where they came from."

A wonderful gesture, indeed. And now, back at the trial, it was time for the prosecutor to go in for the kill.

"Mr. Buckingham, you lied to me at your deposition on January 3rd, 2005. Isn't that true?"

"How so?"

And now we know William Buckingham, or at least the part that's showing.

* * *

To know William Buckingham is to know the millions of our fellow Americans who are ignorant not only of the theory they'd like to discredit, but also of the pseudo-theory with which they'd like to replace it; who, knowing full well that they lack the basic data to make a decision between the two, do so anyway, and loudly at that; and who lie through their teeth when asked exactly what it is that motivates them to do these sorts of things in the first place.

William Buckingham lied because he believed it was necessary to do so in order to preserve the truth as he saw it – that literalized Christianity is the one, true religion, and that Darwinism is its greatest threat. But how did he know what to lie about in the course of the Dover trial? Was Buckingham sophisticated enough to understand the legal complications that would have arisen if his efforts at the school board were to be revealed for what they actually were – not a good-faith attempt to provide students with a better education, but rather a badly-concealed attempt to force his private theology on a public institution?

He most certainly was not. Before a certain point, Buckingham had been careless about expressing his own true feelings in public forums:

"This country wasn't founded on Muslim beliefs or evolution. This country was founded on Christianity and our students should be taught as such."

"I challenge you, the audience, to trace your roots to the monkey you came from."

"Nowhere in the Constitution does it call for the separation of church and state."

"2000 years ago, somebody died on a cross. Can't someone take a stand for him?"

But then, before the trial got underway, William Buckingham received a phone call. The caller gave him some free legal advice, advice which would ultimately be ruled as privileged. From that point on, there would be no more talk of creationism or 2,000-year-old executions or the inferiority of Muslim theology in general or the superiority of "Christian America" in particular. Suddenly, Buckingham had gone from an open advocate of state-sponsored evangelism to a subdued proponent of fair and open scientific debate. Buckingham had learnt that discretion is the better part of valor. Or perhaps "valor" isn't quite the right word.

The call Buckingham had received was from the Discovery Institute, the nation's most prominent organization for the advocacy of Intelligent Design. The aforementioned William Dembski is a senior fellow there. He's also an avid proponent of something called "Christology," which he claims will change science forever.

Welcome to the jungle.

TWO

A Brief History of Nonsense

Do not suppose that I have come to bring peace to the earth. I did not come to bring peace, but a sword. For I have come to turn a man against his father, a daughter against her mother, a daughter-in-law against her mother-in-law – a man's enemies will be the members of his own household.

– Jesus Christ, predicting the culture war in the *Book of Matthew*

"The Prince of Peace."

– Poorly-researched title of William Jennings   Bryan's 1904 speech attacking evolution and reaffirming literal Christianity

Three interesting things occurred towards the end of 2005, 2005 having been a slow year in general. One of these interesting things, which we'll refer to as *Interesting Thing A*, occurred on December 20th, when the U.S. district court overseeing the Dover case ruled against the school district in question and further held that Intelligent Design is not actually, you know, science. *Interesting Thing A* seemed to indicate that Intelligent Design and associated elements of sloppy thinking would never hold up in court.

The other interesting thing, which we might as well call *Interesting Thing B*, had occurred three months previously, during the Senate confirmation hearings for soon-to-be Chief Justice John Roberts. *Interesting Thing B* consists of a brief exchange between Roberts and freshman Senator Tom Coburn, an Oklahoman who first gained national recognition after complaining about the rampant lesbianism that was allegedly occurring in his home state's university bathrooms (yes, Oklahoma has both a university and bathrooms).

When we join them, Tom the Senator and John the Justice are gabbing about the nature of law:

> COBURN: So the only question I would have for you is this one final – and I will finish, I hope, before 10 minutes are consumed. Where'd our law – would you teach the American public where our law came from? I mean, there was law before the American Revolution. Where did our law come from? Where'd it come from?

> ROBERTS: Well, before the revolution, of course, we were under the British legal system.

> COBURN: And before that?

> ROBERTS: We go back under the legal system in Britain to the Magna Carta and the dispute between the king and the lords there, as they tried to establish their rights against the king

or central government, was a key part of the development of English law since that time.

COBURN: And prior to that? But some of the input to that was what some people, these very people who are worried, these very people who have lost confidence, call natural law. The ideas came from somewhere, didn't they? Like, don't kill somebody. Don't steal from them. Be truthful. Where did those come from? Those came from the natural tendencies of what we were taught in beliefs through the years that would best support a society. There is a theological component to that to many people. But the fact is there's a basis for the laws that we have. And it's proven consistent through the years, even as it comes to America, that if we enforce those tenets, we all are better off.

So Tom Coburn asks the soon-to-be Chief Justice of the Supreme Court about the origin of American law. The soon-to-be Chief Justice of the Supreme Court answers him. But Tom Coburn doesn't like the answer. So he provides his own answer, which, in essence, is that American law comes from natural law – in this case, he's obviously referring to the Ten Commandments. The soon-to-be Chief Justice of the Supreme Court smiles politely and says nothing.

Why did John Roberts fail to answer? Perhaps he was too stricken with gratitude to speak. After all, Roberts had certainly spent quite a bit of his life studying the nature of American law, and had even practiced quite a bit of it, but, before now, he had never really had the chance to learn Tom Coburn's opinion. And now, here was Tom Coburn himself, providing Tom Coburn's opinion.

Or perhaps John Roberts didn't answer because he'd

read the Ten Commandments, compared it to American law, and noticed not only a striking lack of similarities, but also an even more striking presence of dissimilarities. Take, for instance, the First Commandment and the First Amendment:

First Commandment: "I am the Lord thy God, who brought you out of the land of Egypt, out of the house of bondage. Thou shalt have no other gods before Me."

First Amendment: "Congress shall make no law respecting an establishment of religion, or prohibiting the free exercise thereof."

To briefly recap, the former demands recognition of a specific religion, and the latter forbids it. And there you have it. The First Commandment violates the First Amendment. Only one commandment into the ten, Tom Coburn's alleged wellspring of American legal thought has already proved unconstitutional.

Or perhaps when Coburn implied that American law derived from the Ten Commandments, he was referring to the sort of law enforced by cops and meter maids – noise ordinances and such things. If so, he would be partly right. After all, the Ten Commandments forbid killing and stealing. And, lo and behold, killing and stealing are currently illegal in most parts of the U.S.

Of course, he would also be partly wrong, or, to put it another way, entirely wrong. The Ten Commandments also forbid any and all labor on the Sabbath, which traditionally refers to Saturday but which Christians changed to Sunday when God wasn't looking. You'll notice, though, that one may still legally patronize a 7 Eleven, or even work at one, during the weekend. Elsewhere, adherents are required to "honor" their fathers and mothers. This is a little vague, but whatever it means, it doesn't seem to correspond to any current U.S. laws, which is why you can still stick your elderly father in a rest home if he starts getting all wacky on you. And then there's "Thou shalt not commit adultery." Watch the Senate pass that one.

So when Tom Coburn asserts that American law is somehow based on the Ten Commandments, he's obviously wrong. When the millions of culturally conservative American voters of the sort that put Tom Coburn in office assert the very same thing, they, too are obviously wrong. And not even the presence of a Republican-nominated Chief Justice of the Supreme Court, who obviously disagrees, can shame them away from trying to pass off such obviously wrong things as obviously factual. This is because they know that they are right. Obviously.

So we have *Interesting Thing A*, which indicates that Intelligent Design won't hold up in court. And then we have *Interesting Thing B*, which indicates that the sort of people who dig Intelligent Design – people like Tom Coburn – also believe that their views are backed by "natural law," which itself consists of whichever Biblical vagaries religious types are digging at any given point in time. And natural law, being natural by nature, naturally applies in all natural circumstances (sorry), even if "man's law" also happens to be in effect.

But what happens when lesser, ephemeral "man's law" collides with superior, eternal "natural law"? This brings us to *Interesting Thing C*, which actually occurred towards the beginning of 2005, on March 18th. On that day, after years of litigation and a whopping fourteen appeals spearheaded by her parents and several pro-life organizations, Terri Schiavo's feeding tube was finally ordered removed by the overseeing court, which had determined – for the fourteenth time, mind you – that Terri Schiavo was in a persistent vegetative state from which recovery was impossible, that she herself would not have chosen to go on in such a state, and that her husband Michael had the legal right to end treatment and allow his wife to die.

But the courts involved made a serious mistake – they failed to take into account the opinion of the hundred million or so Americans whose loyalty is not to the United States, its laws, or its courts, but to God. And not just some Jungian, Unitarian Universalist God that manifests itself through pretty butterflies and a child's laughter or something stupid like that – specifically, their loyalty was to Yahweh. And Yahweh, according to the high priests of the hour, wanted Terri Schiavo to spend another decade or so in a Florida hospital bed, so that her trashy, wacked-out Catholic parents could occasionally come by and apply makeup to her face and take her picture (yes, this actually happened).

Unfortunately, Yahweh can't vote or even lobby. And though He nonetheless had the legal right to make His views known, He never actually got around to it. Luckily, culturally conservative crusader and Focus on the Family kingpin Dr. James Dobson was on hand to express Yahweh's views for him – and Yahweh's views, coincidentally enough, happened to coincide with the views of millions of voters of the sort who can make or break a congressman from a generally conservative district.

So, what did these congressmen do on March 18th, the day that the feeding tube was ordered to be removed? If you don't already know, you'll never guess in a million years.

They subpoenaed Terri Schiavo.

Seriously. Here it is. Read it.

Dear Mrs. Schiavo:

Attached please find a subpoena to appear on Friday, March 25 2005, at 10:00 am, at the Hospice of the Florida Suncoast for the Committee on Government Reform.

The Committee has initiated an inquiry into the long term [sic] care of incapacitated adults, an issue of growing importance to the federal government and federal health care policy. The hearing will review the treatment options provided to incapacitated patients to advance the quality of life by examining the procedures, practices, methods, and equipment used by health care professionals. Additionally, the Committee will examine nutrition and hydration which incapacitated patients receive as part of their care. Further, the Committee seeks to understand the issues raised by the legislative proposals contained in H.R. 1332, Protection of Incapacitated Persons Act of 2005 and S. 539, Incapacitated Persons Legal Protection Act of 2005. Your appearance at the hearing would be central to the Committee's understanding of these matters.

Thank you in advance for your participation in this important hearing. If you have any questions regarding this hearing, please contact the Committee at (202) 225-5074.

Sincerely,
Tom Davis
Chairman

It was certainly nice of Tom the Chairman to include a phone number just in case Schiavo had any questions – questions like, "You know I can't talk, see, hear, or process information, right?"

Actually, they didn't know that. To have known that, they would have had to have taken a single, cursory glance at any written summary of the collective opinions of the dozen or so neurologists who had already figured as much after careful review of Schiavo's condition. But, of course, Tom Davis and his buddies didn't do that. Why would they have? James Dobson of Focus on the Family, Senate Majority Leader Bill Frist, and every single porcelain angel figurine collector in the entire United States had already decided that Schiavo was capable not only of seeing, hearing, talking, and feeling, but also perhaps of someday getting up, walking around, and thanking James Dobson of Focus on the Family, Senate Majority Leader Bill Frist, and every single porcelain angel figurine collector in the country for never losing faith, even in the light of reason.

(By the way, I've purposely left in the phone number

for the House Committee on Government Reform as a public service to anyone reading this who may suspect that they, too, might end up in some sort of intractable medical condition at some point in the future. This way, you can go ahead and call in advance and let the HCGR know how you take your coffee and everything.)

A few months after Schiavo died, the results of the autopsy were released. It turns out that her brain had at some point shrunk by half of its weight, that nearly every region of said brain had suffered severe and irreversible damage, and that, in summation, Terri Schiavo had been totally unaware of her surroundings for fifteen long years. Not in a Courtney Love sort of way, but rather in an actual, literal, medical sort of way.

Only a few weeks earlier, James Dobson had suggested on his website that Terri would have enjoyed "an outing at a mall," and criticized Michael Schiavo for having discouraged such activities when her parents had proposed them.

And though James Dobson was the more formally recognized leader of the religious backlash, it was then-House Majority Leader Tom DeLay who managed to strike the more Abrahamic tone of the two, announcing after Schiavo's death that "the time will come for the men responsible for this to answer for their behavior." When later asked exactly what he meant by this, DeLay explained that "it means there are a lot of questions." Quick note to any restaurant waiters who may have the bad fortune to serve Tom DeLay – if he tells you, apropos of nothing, that "the time will come for you to answer for your behavior," what he really means is that he has a lot of questions about the menu, like what the soup of the day is and whether the resident pasta is Atkins-friendly.

Now, let's review:

Interesting Thing A: Intelligent Design and associated elements of sloppy thinking will never hold up in court.

Interesting Thing B: The sort of people who dig Intelligent Design (see Tom Coburn) also believe that their views are backed by "natural law," which itself consists of whichever Biblical vagaries religious types are digging at any given point in time.

Interesting Thing C: When "natural law" and "man's law" collide, certain advocates of "natural law" are perfectly willing to intervene to whatever extent they deem possible, including but not limited to subpoenaing invalids, threatening the judiciary, and otherwise engaging in various acts of wholesale tomfoolery.

Which is to say, advocates of natural law will never really accept any court decision regarding evolution that they deem to be contrary to their own personal beliefs. But just for fun, let's go over a few of them anyway.

* * *

In 1859, Charles Darwin published *On the Origin of Species by Means of Natural Selection, or the Preservation of Favoured Races in the Struggle for Life*, this being the catchiest title he could think of at the time. And though Darwin wasn't the first Western intellectual to speculate that the wide variety of species we see today are the result of some sort of understandable naturalistic mechanism, he was certainly the first to popularize the idea.

Just a year after publication, *Origin* had already created such a stir that the organizers of the British Association for the Advancement of Science opted to dedicate much of their next annual blowout to the concept of natural selection and the implications thereof. And so it came to be that the event schedule would be the most action-packed in recent memory. On Thursday, for instance, attendees would attend a lecture in which the brain structures of apes and humans would be compared and contrasted, and on Friday, a paper would be presented on the embryonic development of sea squirt eggs. But it never seemed to occur to the organizers that two days spent thusly might be just too much damned excitement for a bunch of Victorian Englanders, and so, instead of allowing for a cooling off period, they went ahead and scheduled for Saturday a grand debate between Thomas Henry Huxley, the noted biologist and professional lecturer who had previously serenaded attendees with tales of primate brains and sea squirt eggs (and who had himself coined the term "agnosticism"), and Samuel Wilberforce, a prominent bishop known otherwise as "Soapy Sam" for his notorious ability to avoid being pinned down in an argument.

Incidentally, what has since been referred to as the Huxley-Wilberforce debate was never actually scheduled as such – instead, it sort of evolved (sorry again) out of what was originally planned as a general presentation by Huxley on the scientific virtues of Darwin's volume, with the format allowing for a sort of informal, back-and-forth argument between Huxley and several other participants who would then be allowed to refute him. After these several participants had done just that, the audience called for Wilberforce to speak as well. This was rather convenient, as Wilberforce just happened to be sitting on stage at that very moment, having been blessed with a choice seat due to his status as vice-president of the very association that holds the conference.

Wilberforce began his oration with a general attack on Darwin's much-touted bestseller. This didn't go so well, as the good bishop was evidently a little unclear on the finer points of the book. But what Wilberforce lacked in understanding he more than made up for in *cojones*; at one point, he famously asked Huxley whether the latter's personal descent from apes could be traced through his grandfather or his grandmother. This being the sort of sexless time and place in which the nickname

"Soapy Sam" would not immediately be recognized as at least five or six double-entendres, Wilberforce had consequently violated an unwritten Victorian custom which precluded the suggestion of bestiality on the part of one's grandparents, particularly in mixed company. In fact, at least one woman present was reported to have fainted, fainting still having been in fashion at the time.

Seeing an opening, Huxley moved to win sympathy from the audience while concurrently taking a swipe at the good bishop. As Huxley himself later recounted:

> "[I had] listened with great attention to the Lord Bishop's speech but had been unable to discern either a new fact or a new argument in it – except indeed the question raised as to my personal predilection in the matter of ancestry – that it would not have occurred to me to bring forward such a topic as that for discussion myself, but that I was quite ready to meet the Right Rev. prelate even on that ground. If then, said I the question is put to me would I rather have a miserable ape for a grandfather or a man highly endowed by nature and possessed of great means of influence and yet who employs these faculties and that influence for the mere purpose of introducing ridicule into a grave scientific discussion, I unhesitatingly affirm my preference for the ape."

Zing! Sort of.

At any rate, Huxley's allegedly witty retort – coupled with a total lack of tact and expertise on the part of the "Lord Bishop" – ensured that the world's first self-proclaimed agnostic would ultimately be viewed as the winner. And thirteen years later, when Wilberforce died from severe head trauma after falling from his horse, Huxley was said to have noted that his old opponent's mind had finally come into contact with reality. Finally, a little pith.

Though obviously not a court case itself, the Huxley-Wilberforce debate may be considered to be a sort of archetype for the formal trials that would come to litter 20th century American history. The whole "Can you trace your ancestry to an ape" shtick, for instance, has since become a staple gag of the creationist crowd, most likely due to a general lack of comedic ingenuity on their part. Perhaps more importantly, though, the fateful encounter of 1860 provided another far more universal precedent: whenever an evolutionist debates a creationist, the creationist will inevitably come off as something of an ill-informed jackass. And if this sounds unfair to creationists, consider William Jennings Bryan.

* * *

Wanna learn a neat trick? Well, of course you do. It only works for males, though. Sorry, ladies!

First, marry anti-feminist icon Phyllis Schlafly, assuming she's still alive (I'm too busy to check) and single (ditto). Then, command her to publicly advocate the Equal Rights Amendment. When she refuses, read her the following verse from the *Book of Genesis*:

"And thy desire shall be to thy husband, and he shall rule over thee."

Uh, oh! Looks like poor Phyllis Schlafly is in your power – orders from the Big Guy himself. And be sure to remind her that, divorce being unholy, she's stuck with you forever. But divorce her anyway, because, you know, *ick*.

Heck, a literal reading of the Bible indicates you can

marry Phyllis Schlafly and Jane Fonda at the very same time, assuming Jane Fonda is down for a little swinging (which is likely), and not currently married to some rich yahoo from the sticks (which is considerably less likely). The *Genesis* figure Lamach, for instance, had two wives, and Yahweh not only approved of the setup, but even blessed the lucky fellow with two sons. Perhaps Yahweh will bless you with two sons, as well, each of whom will presumably marry two more women (some poor sucker out there, less pious than yourself, is probably cursed with a bunch of daughters he's trying to marry off). All of this will result in plenty of grandchildren. You can read them stories from *Genesis*. Here's a good one, from the beginning of Chapter VI:

> "And it came to pass, when men began to multiply on the face of the Earth, and daughters were born unto them, that the sons of God saw the daughters of men that they were fair; and they took them wives of all which they chose... There were giants in the earth in those days; and also after that, when the sons of God came in unto the daughters of men, and they bare children to them, the same became mighty men which were of old, men of renown."

Giants and demigods cross-breeding with earth women to create a new race of super beings who have since vanished without a trace! What kid wouldn't enjoy that?

Being a child at heart, Jane Fonda will probably want to be read a story, too. She'll like this one, from *James V*:

> "Now listen, you rich people, weep and wail because of the misery that is coming upon you. Your wealth has rotted, and moths have eaten your clothes. Your gold and silver are corroded.

> Their corrosion will testify against you and eat
> your flesh like fire."

Bob Dylan owes quite a bit to ol' James. So does Cesar Chavez, as it turns out:

> "Look! The wages you failed to pay the work-
> men who mowed your fields are crying out
> against you! The cries of the harvesters have
> reached the ears of the Lord Almighty!"

Not the sort of stuff that's going to get you on the board of the Federalist Society, to be sure. But if ever in the course of your short, ironic, practical joke of a marriage, Phyllis Schlafly ever wonders aloud, "Whence the source of all this godless communism?" read from the *Book of James*, and politely suggest that the godless communism of Karl Marx may very well derive from the same source as the god-fearing populism of William Jennings Bryan.

Also, be sure you get her to sign a pre-nup.

* * *

William Jennings Bryan may have been an ill-informed jackass, but at least he was a lovable one. Known as "The Great Commoner" for his lifelong backing of populist causes, Bryan was the sort of fellow who could boil down complex economic issues into simple religious ones. This came in handy during his three presidential campaigns, though not so handy that he actually won any of them.

When the election of 1900 pitted mostly Western advocates of "free silver" against mostly Eastern advocates of the gold standard, the silverite Bryan made clear in his speech to the Democratic National Convention that, Dostoevsky to the contrary, Jesus would have preferred to rise again in the West:

> "Having behind us the producing masses of this nation and the world, supported by the commercial interests, the laboring interests and the toilers everywhere, we will answer their demand for a gold standard by saying to them: You shall not press down upon the brow of labor this crown of thorns, you shall not crucify mankind upon a cross of gold!"

Having said his piece, Bryan then stretched his arms out to both sides in an imitation of Christ on the cross. The crowd went wild – having nothing better to do.

Subtlety was not one of Bryan's strong suits. His campaign poster from that same election depicted, among other things, a sort of Lady Liberty archetype attacking a giant octopus with an axe. The octopus, of course, represented the industrial trusts, and thus the image was not to be taken literally. Unlike the Bible, which was. Except when it wasn't. A quarter century after his Cross of Gold campaign, when Bryan volunteered to serve as the prosecutor for the Scopes Trial, he got to learn all sorts of neat stuff about what exactly it was he personally believed about the Bible. This was thanks to defense attorney Clarence Darrow, who, as we shall see, was nice enough to hold his hand through the whole theological mess.

The Scopes Trial's celebrated Bryan/Darrow confrontation was a match made in Clichéd Conflict Heaven. In contrast to the pious, traditional-minded Bryan, Clarence Darrow was perfectly emblematic of the secular, modernist, semi-deterministic moral relativists who were just then coming into vogue (and who still serve as a sort of eternal fundraising tool for the Christian Right to this very day). In fact, at the time when the Scopes Trial began, Darrow had just completed his most celebrated feat of secular, modernist, semi-deterministic moral relativism to date, having managed to save two of his clients from the death penalty against all odds.

The case involved two young men, Loeb and Leopold, who had previously confessed to the "thrill-killing" of a 14 year-old boy. Aside from being Jewish – and thus implicitly guilty of the "thrill-killing" of Jesus, too – the two defendants were homosexuals to boot, and it was a hell of a break for Darrow when he managed to keep both of these juicy pieces of gossip out of the courtroom, if not the newspapers.

Darrow's bid for leniency at the trial revolved around the still-novel idea that environmental factors – in this case, too much German philosophy and too little sense – should be regarded as extenuating, at least when it came down to matters of punishment. And in arguing for the relatively light punishment of life in prison, Darrow had even held that the family of the victim should feel sorry for the families of the accused, as the families of the accused were being subjected to far greater degrees of suffering than anyone else involved in the case. In short, it would have been difficult to come up with someone more inflammatory to the sensibilities of conservative America than this early 20th century Honky Johnny Cochran.

The events leading up to the Scopes Trial were rather less disturbing than those leading up to Darrow's previous legal engagement, unless you happen to be easily disturbed by stupid laws that obviously violate both the spirit and letter of the First Amendment, in which case you might want to get yourself a security blanket and a glass of warm milk or something before reading further. The stupid law in question was the Butler Act, passed by the Tennessee state legislature on March 21, 1925, which deemed it unlawful...

> "...for any teacher in any of the Universities, Normals and all other public schools of the state – which are supported in whole or in part by the public school funds of the State, to teach

any theory that denies the story of the Divine Creation of man as taught in the Bible, and to teach instead that man has descended from a lower order of animals."

What made the Butler Act notable in a nation already plagued with state anti-evolution measures was the fact that this particular law made the teaching of evolution a crime, to be punishable by a fine. Enter the ACLU, which had been itching for a fight on the teaching of evolution for years, and which immediately began running an ad in Tennessee newspapers, which read in part:

"We are looking for a Tennessee teacher who is willing to accept our services in testing this law in the courts. Our lawyers think a friendly test can be arranged without costing the teacher his or her job. Distinguished counsel have volunteered their services. All we need is a willing client."

Not only did they find a willing client, but also a willing locale. The civic leaders of Dayton, Tennessee, totally dug the idea of turning their little town into a makeshift cultural battleground; every army fights on its stomach after all, and an army of big city lawyers may be expected to dine without regard to expense. Not only would a trial bring in cash, the town leaders reasoned, but perhaps it would even put little Dayton on the map. And in the end, it did.

Having decided in favor of a circus, Dayton's civic leaders encouraged a young school teacher by the name of John Thomas Scopes to serve as clown-bait. And although young Scopes couldn't actually recall ever having taught evolution, he had indeed assigned his students a state approved textbook which dealt with the subject. And thus the stage was set for a goofy, media-friendly sham trial that would ultimately solve nothing whatsoever.

Though he hadn't argued a case in decades, William Jennings Bryan leaped at the chance to serve as prosecutor. And having grown accustomed to a less formal sort of demagoguery in those intervening, politically active years, Bryan brought to the trial a level of intellectual rigor one might expect from a guy in the habit of blithely comparing sound monetary policy to the crucifixion of Jesus – throughout the trial Bryan spoke with his back to the judge in order to better rile up the gallery. He was also fond of throwing out such empty pronouncements as, "Darwinism is not science at all; it is a string of guesses strung together. There is more science in the twenty-fourth verse of the first chapter of *Genesis*... than in all that Darwin wrote."

In case you're wondering what that allegedly science-packed Bible verse may consist of, here it is:

> "And God said, 'Let the land produce living creatures according to their kinds: livestock, creatures that move along the ground, and wild animals, each according to its kind.' And it was so."

Suck on that, methodological naturalism! But while such utterances of faith are good, true, and gosh-darned apple pie-ish in the hands of a Christian, they apparently take on a sillier aspect when (allegedly) applied by scientists; Bryan also claimed that Darwinism "requires more faith in chance than a Christian is required to have in God." If this were true – and, incidentally, it is not – it would ironically make scientists the most faithful people on the planet. Irony being generally lost on the pious, it would never occur to Bryan or anyone else of his ilk that to praise one's own extent of faith while criticizing others for having too much faith reveals a subtle, unconscious realization that too much faith is a disability which prevents access to the truth. In fact, the "Darwinism-as-faith" meme is still a popular rhetorical tactic among anti-evolutionists to this very day.

Being a populist at heart, Bryan also made a point of defending the mentality behind the Butler Act; namely, that taxpayers or their representatives should be permitted to "control the schools which they create and support." This, too, remains an important argument on the part of anti-evolutionists, and will undoubtedly remain so until some community of sarcastic, trouble-making atheists decide that local public schools should teach that Jesus was actually a space alien. The ball's in your court, Berkley.

But of all the arguments presented by Bryan in defense of literalist Christianity over godless evolution, perhaps the most popularly effective was the one he took from Darrow's own mouth. During the Loeb/Leopold Trial, Darrow had defended the older of the two boys thusly:

> "This terrible crime was inherent in his organism, and it came from some ancestor… Is any blame attached because somebody took Nietzsche's philosophy seriously and fashioned his life upon it? … It is hardly fair to hang a 19 year-old boy for the philosophy that was taught him at the university."

Darrow, Bryan pointed out, had spent the previous year making excuses for two murderers on the strength that they had picked up an amoral philosophy in the course of their education, taken it seriously, and then acted on it. And now, this year, here was Darrow again, attempting to legitimatize yet another apparently amoral philosophy. Certainly the widespread teaching of evolution could lead to nothing less than an entire nation dotted with latter-day Loebs and Leopolds.

Today, we can confirm that this is hardly the case by visiting any American prison and noting the conspicuous rarity of philosophy majors and grad students incarcerated therein. But Bryan's argument was far more understandable in 1925, without the benefit of hindsight – or, at least, it would have been, assuming he knew as little about the violent history of Christianity as he did about the basics of economics. And we can probably go ahead and assume that, too.

But no matter how little Bryan may have known about his religion's history, he certainly didn't seem to know much about origins, either. This was confirmed when Bryan – not to be outdone by a well-received speech given by Darrow's fellow defense attorney Dudley Field Malone – insisted on taking the witness stand so that Darrow could cross-examine him regarding the Bible, thus giving Bryan the chance to yet again hear the sound of his own voice. It may not have been a good move on the part of Bryan, who claimed he was acting " not for the benefit of the superior court," but rather to "keep these gentlemen from saying I was afraid to meet them and let them question me, and I want the Christian world to know that any atheist, agnostic, unbeliever, can question me anytime as to my belief in God, and I will answer him." This was technically true, as Darrow the agnostic could indeed question Bryan as to his belief in God, and Bryan did indeed answer him. But Darrow, like most skeptics who have read the Bible, was an accomplished smart-ass, and his questions to Bryan – like where exactly it was that Cain got his wife from when he and his brother Able theoretically made up the entire second generation of humanity, for instance – ended up having the effect, as Bryan put it then, "to cast ridicule on everybody who believes in the Bible."

In the end, no one really got what they wanted from the Scopes Trial. The ACLU's intent had been to lose the case and work an appeal up to the U.S. Supreme Court, thus making the world safe for evolutionary theory; instead, they had to settle for a single appeal, which only had the effect of determining that the $100 fine applied on Scopes (after all, he was guilty) was illegitimate, as the judge in question wasn't authorized to fine anyone more than $50. Apparently, it took the Tennessee Supreme Court to figure this out. As for William Jennings Bryan, he died five days after the trial, so he probably never did get a chance to figure out where Cain had gotten that damned wife of his.

But from the standpoint of the humanist crowd, maybe a little good did come from the publicity surrounding the Scopes Trial. After 1925, the legislatures of twenty southern states suddenly developed a very strong interest in science. Unfortunately, this was the same sort of interest that a Viking berserker develops for a comely young maiden whose village he's just burned to the ground; of the twenty state evolution laws passed over the next few years, a full twenty of them were dedicated to criminalizing the teaching of Darwin's works.

Unsurprisingly, one of these laws was passed in Arkansas, in 1928. Three years having passed since Scopes, the anti-evolutionist forces were a bit more specific when they prohibited teachers...

> "...in any university, college, normal, public school, or other institution of the state, which is supported in whole or in part from public funds derived by state and local taxation, to teach the theory or doctrine that mankind ascended or descended from a lower order of animals... any teacher or other instructor or textbook commissioner who is found guilty of violation of this act... shall be guilty of a misdemeanor and upon conviction shall vacate the position thus held in any educational institution above mentioned."

In short: push evolution in a public capacity and you'll never work in Arkansas again. This wasn't much of a threat to anyone who's ever had the opportunity to find themselves working in Arkansas, which may explain why state textbook commissioners totally disregarded the law when they approved a 1965 high school biology textbook containing a chapter on evolution.

Enter Susan Epperson, a biology teacher who migrated to Arkansas as a military wife and who was probably none too happy to be there in the first place. In a legal sense, Epperson had a pretty good reason to challenge the 1928 statute – after all, her contract required her to teach all recognized branches of biology, and by 1965, evolution was very recognized indeed, biologists having failed to consult the Arkansas legislature before deciding this.

Unlike the eight-day blowout in Tennessee, *Epperson v. Arkansas* took a scant two hours, after which the judge in question ruled that the Arkansas statute was indeed unconstitutional, and that the teaching of evolution wasn't "a hazard to the health and morals of the community." This last point must have been particularly important to a state that consistently ranks in the bottom echelons of every health measurement known to man, and which also produced that utter paragon of old-fashioned morality, Bill Clinton.

But the Arkansas Supreme Court, which apparently exists, disagreed, declaring that the law had indeed been constitutional and was also "a valid exercise of the state's own power to specify the curriculum in its public schools." And thus it was time for the final arbiters of all that is good and true to step in and make a decision. But since television punditry was still in its infancy, America had to settle for the U.S. Supreme Court.

One of the justices, Abe Fortas, had been a 15 year-old Tennessee resident at the time of the Scopes Trial. Suitably embarrassed by the antics of his fellow southerners during that controversy and this one as well, Fortas issued a far-reaching unanimous decision which got to the heart of the matter:

"The appeal challenges the constitutionality of the 'anti-evolution' statute which the state of Arkansas adopted in 1928 to prohibit the teaching in its public schools and universities of the theory that man evolved from other species of life. The statute was a product of the upsurge of 'fundamentalist' religious fervor of the twenties. The Arkansas statute was an adaptation of the famous Tennessee 'Monkey Law' which that state adopted in 1925...The overriding fact is that the Arkansas law selects from the body of knowledge a particular segment which it proscribes for the sole reason that it is deemed to conflict with a particular religious doctrine, that is, with a particular interpretation of the *Book of Genesis* by a particular group."

Or, as the court later summed it up, "the state has no legitimate interest in protecting any or all religions from views distasteful to them."

Amen.

THREE

Dinosaurs & Exclamation Marks

Many people have gone to Mt. Ararat to try to find Noah's Ark. I have been there more than ten times.

– John D. Morris, scientific creationist and apparent boon to the Turkish economy

This reminds me of a man who wanted to sell me a secret method of communicating with a person two or three thousand miles away, by means of a certain sympathy of magnetic needles. I told him that I would gladly buy, but wanted to see by experiment, and that it would be enough for me if he would stand in one room, and I in another. He replied that its operation could not be detected at such a short distance. I sent him on his way, with the remark that I was not in the mood at that time to go to Cairo or Moscow for the experiment, but that if he wanted to go I would stay in Venice and take care of the other end.

– Galileo Galilei, *Dialogue Concerning the Two Chief World Systems*

George McCready Price, who may be considered the illegitimate father of that bastard "discipline" known as "scientific creationism," set the intellectual tone for the movement in his unfortunately influential 1935 work, "The Modern Flood Theory of Geology," in which he makes the following pronouncement:

> "Evolution, forsooth! Why, in every case where we can come to actual grips with the facts, there is absolute evidence of degeneracy, not evolution."

Zounds! Balderdash! Humbug!

The first thing one should know about Price (aside from the fact that he was in the habit of using terms like "forsooth" and dotting his prose with exclamation marks) is that before he began writing "young-earth creationist" textbooks, he first failed as a preacher. How one manages to fail at a job which requires no tangible results is a great mystery, on par with the origin of Cain's wife.

On the other hand, the denomination to which Price was born into – and which Price thus assumed to be the one, true faith, because, after all, he was born into it – was the Seventh-Day Adventist Church, which itself stemmed from the mid-19th century "Millerite Movement," named for farmer-theologian William Miller. Miller's most notable contribution to Christian thought was his pseudo-mathematical prediction that Christ would return in 1843. This, uh, didn't turn out to be the case. And so perhaps one could forgive a fellow for failing as an Adventist preacher, in the same sense that one can forgive another fellow for failing as an Amway salesman. "Castles built on sand," you know.

But on the third hand (I'm deformed), the obvious limitations of this particular denomination didn't stop Adventist-off-shoot David Koresh from becoming one of the most successful preachers in history, second only to Jesus himself. The highest form of recognition a preacher can receive is to gain the attention of a world superpower – whether it be Rome or America – and to then be killed by agents of said empire – whether it be Pontius Pilate or Janet Reno. Two thousand years from now, Latino youths will no doubt be sporting golden necklaces with little flammable gas canister symbols affixed to them in recognition of that glorious day when David Koresh died for the sins of the ATF.

At any rate, when the Millerites noticed that 1843 had come and gone with no sign of the Second Coming – and one tends to notice things like the dead rising from their graves and stretching their legs a bit – they promptly changed their story. Miller's calculations, they decided, had indeed been spot on, but Miller had accidentally calculated the year in which Jesus was to begin his "investigative judgment" of the world – from heaven, conveniently enough. And such was the proud intellectual tradition that would later give the world George McCready Price.

Let's take another look at that quote:

"Evolution, forsooth! Why, in every case where we can come to actual grips with the facts, there is absolute evidence of degeneracy, not evolution."

Poppycock! Flimflam! Great Caesar's ghost!

Apologies. So what is this "absolute evidence of degeneracy" that McCready had discovered? Why, the observation that, according to the fossil record, many species seem to have gotten smaller, not larger, over the years. Small organisms, you see, are "degenerate." This would certainly explain the presidency of George W. Bush, who, at 5'11", is one of our smaller, more "degenerate" presidents. But it certainly doesn't explain Gerald Ford, who, at 6'2", was one of the tallest presidents in modern history, and thus, according to McCready's "reasoning," should have been remembered as one of the greatest Americans of all time, as opposed to just a guy who fell down a lot.

Aside from his arbitrary contention that larger is better (you've probably noticed how well the brontosauruses are doing these days), McCready's central anti-evolution argument is doubly silly when one also notices that McCready denies the legitimacy of the fossil record itself. To make this is a bit clearer:

McCready Assertion A: The fossil record shows that species have gotten smaller over the years.

McCready Assertion B: The fossil record is incorrect.

And from there, the scientific creationism movement continues to "degenerate."

Decades after McCready's death, proponents of young-earth pseudoscience still cling to their intellectual forbearer's contention that the world's species have somehow weakened over the years. Incapable of finding any real evidence of this, but quite capable of ignoring all evidence to the contrary, many post-McCready creationists have instead resorted to a willful misunderstanding of the Second Law of Thermodynamics, which holds that, in a closed system, complexity tends to dissolve into uniformity, or entropy. In other words, a system that receives no outside energy will eventually dissipate as existing energy diffuses.

Creationists have seized upon this law as proof that evolution cannot occur – after all, they say, if entropy is always increasing, then complex organisms can hardly be expected to arise out of simpler ones, and in fact the opposite must be true. Or, as prominent creation scientist Henry Morris once put it, the laws of science are "laws of conservation and deterioration, not of creation and integration."

This would be a hell of an argument against evolution (and many other things) if the Earth was a closed system – which, incidentally, it is not. The large orb that appears in the sky each day, for instance, provides light and heat to the planet, making Earth an open system, and thus not subject as a unit to the Second Law of Thermodynamics. This rather important condition to the law explains...well, it explains pretty much everything, like why seeds grow into plants instead of simply rotting, or why babies grow into adults instead of simply dying on the spot, or why any organism is capable of existing for any period of time whatsoever.

At some point, this concept was finally explained to Henry Morris and others of his ilk, all of whom promptly apologized for having failed to understand basic scientific principles while simultaneously claiming to be the greatest scientists in the world. Just kidding. In 1985, Henry Morris responded to his scientific critics thusly:

> "Although it is true that the two laws of thermo-dynamics are defined in terms of isolated systems, it is also true that in the real world there is no such thing as an isolated system. All systems in reality are open systems and, furthermore, they are all open in greater or lesser degree, directly or indirectly, to the energy from the sun. Therefore, to say that the earth is a system open to the sun's energy does not explain anything, since the same statement is true for every other system as well!"

Well, it certainly doesn't explain the widespread addiction to exclamation marks among scientific creationists (and one can't help but imagine what the withdrawal would be like). But it actually does explain several other things, like why the Second Law of Thermodynamics doesn't preclude evolution from occurring on earth, which, as Henry Morris seems to have conveniently forgotten, is what he and his buddies were originally asserting, and which is how the Second Law of Thermodynamics originally came into the wider discussion in the first place. But Henry Morris is correct that there are no truly isolated systems in reality. The concept of an isolated system is simply a useful model for explaining other processes too wonkish to go into here.

How can creation scientists be so damned wrong about concepts that can easily be explained in laymen's terms? Because they feel like it. To the average creation scientist, science is only valid if it backs up what the creation scientist has already accepted to be true. For example, take a look at the submission guidelines of the *Creation Ex Nihilo Technical Journal*, an important foundation of creation science published by the, er, Creation Science Foundation:

> • The Bible is the written Word of God. It is divinely inspired throughout.
> • The final guide to the interpretation of Scripture is Scripture itself.
> • The account of origin presented in *Genesis* is a simple but factual presentation of actual events and therefore provides a reliable framework for scientific research into the question of the origin and history of life, mankind, the earth and the universe.
> • Scripture teaches a recent origin for man and the whole creation.
> • The great flood of *Genesis* was an actual historic event, worldwide (global) in its extent and effect.
> • The special creation of Adam (as one man) and Eve (as one woman) and their subsequent fall into sin, is the basis for the necessity of salvation for

mankind (and thus for the Gospel of Jesus Christ).

• The scientific aspects of creation are important, but are secondary in importance to the proclamation of the Gospel of Jesus Christ as Sovereign, Creator, Redeemer and Judge.

Gee, tough crowd. And God help the poor son of a bitch whose submission alludes to Jesus Christ as only the Sovereign, Creator, and Redeemer, but not Judge. Or Judge, Sovereign, and Redeemer, but not Creator. Coptics need not apply.

But as fond as creationists are of their own intricate, *a priori* dogma, they're even fonder of accusing actual scientists of being dogmatic themselves. Here's a quote from Ken Ham, a prominent creation scientist whom we'll have occasion to beat up on several times throughout the course of this book:

> "Creationists, of course, would not be surprised if someone found a living dinosaur. However, evolutionists would then have to explain why they made dogmatic statements that man and dinosaur never lived at the same time."

Actually, both of these statements are correct. Creationists would indeed not be surprised if someone found a living dinosaur. Nor would a six year-old child or a schizophrenic be all that shocked, for that matter. And neither creationist nor six year-old child nor schizophrenic nor six year-old schizophrenic creationist would be all that surprised if suddenly there appeared in the sky four great beasts covered in eyeballs, possessing six wings each, and resembling a lion, a calf, a man, and an eagle, respectively, and if the appearance of said beasts was quickly followed by a voice proclaiming, "A measure of wheat for a penny, and three measures of barley for a penny, and see thou hurt not the oil and wine," and if each beast opened a seal, and if out of the fourth seal came a pale horse ridden by Death, and if Death was then given power over a fourth of the Earth's inhabitants, "to kill with sword, and with hunger, and with death *[which one might think would be sort of implied]*, and with the beasts of the Earth," and if the stars then fell unto the Earth while oddly not destroying it completely, and if seven angels also appeared around this time, and if the fifth of these angels was given the key to a bottomless pit, and if the fifth angel then opened the aforementioned pit in order to release giant locusts shaped like horses but with faces of men and the hair of women and breastplates of iron and wings that sounded like the rushing of chariots and tails like scorpions and no apparent locust-like characteristics to speak of even though they're referred to as "locusts" for some stupid reason or another, and if these pseudo-locusts were then commanded by the angel to attack men but not kill them so that they might suffer longer, and then if the sixth angel was commanded to release four more god-damned angels from the bottom of the Euphrates, and then if these four angels were ordered to kill the third of humanity that hadn't already been, you know, crushed by all of those fucking stars, and if things just got weirder from there. They wouldn't be surprised at any of this, because it's spelled out quite specifically in the *Book of Revelation*, and, as we all know per the submission guidelines of *Creation Ex Nihilo Technical Journal,* "the Bible is the written word of God...divinely inspired throughout," and God knows, so to speak, that the creationists can't wait for all this to happen to the rest of us, because then there'll be nobody around to point out that the Second Law of Thermodynamics only applies to closed systems.

But evolutionists, by contrast, would probably be a little surprised. After all, they're a "dogmatic" bunch.

* * *

Incidentally, Ken Ham has yet to find a living dinosaur. There could be any number of reasons for this. Perhaps God is hiding the dinosaurs from him in order to test his faith. Maybe Ken Ham is totally wrong about everything, and dinosaurs died out tens of millions of years ago (Hey, you never know).

But there's also another possibility. Perhaps there are oodles of dinosaurs running around all over the damned place, but the creationists are too incompetent, dishonest, and down-right under-qualified to find them. And in support of this latter theory, I give you the strange case of the Paluxy River Tracks.

Down by the little town of Glen Rose, Texas, you'll find a stretch of the Paluxy River that's famous for two things: tubing, which is a sort of hick-friendly version of sailing; and several specimens of dinosaur tracks, the viewing of which is a sort of equally hick-friendly version of going to a museum or reading a book. The presence of both tubing and dinosaur tracks are indisputable – the tracks have been confirmed a number of times by scientists of both the real and self-proclaimed variety, and the signs around the area clearly state that one may indeed rent a tube (or bring your own if you're a real aficionado), place the tube in the river, carefully work one's way into the tube, and then float said tube down the river while drinking beer and yell-ing at one's obnoxious, overweight kids. This much is clear to everyone concerned, or at least within earshot.

Opinions diverge, though, over another alleged Glenn Rose attraction: other, more ambiguous tracks dating to the same general time period and which appear to be human, at least to the layman or the average creation scientist. Indeed, the tracks have been heralded from some quarters as evidence that man and dinosaur once lived side-by-side ever since they were first discovered about a century ago. In reality, though, the "man tracks" are so questionable that even a few creationists have cast doubt on them, including several researchers from the relatively honest-minded Creationist Research Society.

Nor was the CRS the only creationist institution to even-tually give up on the Paluxy tracks – at least for a little while. In the mid-80s, an amateur paleontologist by the name of Glen

Kuban invited representatives of another group, the Institute for Creation Research, to take another look at the supposed man tracks, and was able to convince them that what appeared at first glance to be the result of giant human feet was actually a product of metatarsal dinosaur feet – which is to say, they were made by a class of dinosaurs who walked on their heels at least part of the time. Disappointed but honest, the ICR members involved later released an article confirming that the tracks in question were "obviously dinosaurian," and that "none of the four trails at the Taylor Site can be today regarded as unquestionably human." By this time, other, more conventional scientists had already discredited the tracks anyway, noting that some had been treated with oil in past photographs in order to bring out certain features, that others were the demonstrable product of natural erosive forces, and that many of them were indeed metatarsal.

Now, one might reasonably suppose that, having released a statement to the effect that the tracks in question cannot be regarded as "unquestionably human," and in fact have been shown to be "obviously dinosaurian," the ICR would consequently refrain from stating otherwise in the future. One would be wrong. And one could be forgiven for being wrong on this point, because one might be unaware that the ICR was founded and operated by disingenuous dumbass Henry Morris, who, as you may recall from above, is a disingenuous dumbass.

And thus it is that even today, about twenty years after the ICR itself confirmed that the tracks are hardly the real deal, you can still log on to the ICR website and read that "many scientists and laymen alike are waking up to the fact that much solid scientific evidence exists that contradicts evolutionary notions," and that "[O]ne of the most shattering pieces of evidence comes from the Paluxy River basin in central Texas, near the town of Glen Rose, where fossilized tracks of man and dinosaur appear together."

And what about those poor, misguided souls who dispute this, like the ICR's own 80s-era investigators? Just ask

Henry Morris' son John, who has since taken over the operations of the ICR and who wrote a few years later that "anti-creationists have devoted an inordinate amount of attention to this project, often ignoring, ridiculing, and distorting the evidence as reported by creationists." A real chip off the ol' block, that John Morris.

So, oddly enough, the efforts of this father-son dynamic duo have actually gone a long way towards showing that dinosaurs might still exist. After all, the only people looking for dinosaurs are creationists, and creationists appear to have bad memories. So, for all we know, Henry and John Morris have already found a dinosaur. But, at some point since then, they just plumb forgot.

Or would it be unfair to suppose that the Morris boys are only in the habit of forgetting things they'd rather not remember in the first place?

* * *

Even more central to the views of creationists than dinosaurs is the Great Flood, which is why the premier crop of creation scientists originally referred to themselves as "flood geologists" instead of, say, "anti-Enlightenment miscreants" or "misguided Levant fetishists" or "mediocre-minded theocrat fodder" or something accurate like that. Admittedly, all of those suggested terms are a bit unwieldy, so let's just call them flood geologists.

Anyway, attempting to explain how the entire planet was covered with thousands of feet of water just a few thousand years ago when the evidence accumulated by dozens of scientific disciplines clearly demonstrates otherwise is no small task. But the creationists are certainly up to it, having discovered a rather effective strategy: ignore all evidence to the contrary, make up implausible and occasionally impossible scenarios for which there is no evidence at all, and, when that doesn't work, simply evoke supernatural intervention on the part of Yahweh, all the while criticizing real scientists for failing to take them seriously. And by "effective strategy," I'm referring to the sense in which closing your eyes and hoping for the best is an "effective strategy" for birth control.

To list all of the scientific and even common-sense reasons why the *Genesis* Flood concept is ludicrous in light of what we know about the world today – as well as the goofy ways in which creationists try to get around this unfortunate circumstance – would be as difficult a chore as, say, building a giant ark and then packing two representatives of each and every one of the millions of animals and insects onto it and then shepherding each and every one of these species back to their appropriate stomping grounds while simultaneously – but then, we're getting ahead of ourselves.

At any rate, although it would be impractical to list all the accumulated nonsense inherent in this particular worldview, it would be a shame not to glance at a sampling, because it's actually pretty funny stuff. And so, in no particular order of importance, let us examine the silly explanations that creationists have come up with for the *Genesis* Flood, Noah's ark, and even the "UFO phenomenon."

That's right. We're gonna go nuts here.

PROFILES IN STUPIDITY:
A Reasonable Person's Guide to Unreasonable Bullshit

Water

According to the *Book of Genesis* – and thus, according to creation scientists as well – the great flood which God caused to occur for some reason or another was so massive in scale that it covered even the top of Mount Ararat, which the Bible clearly states was under water at the time. A flood of such a degree would have had to involve four and a half times the amount of water currently present on the planet. The obvious question, then, concerns where all this water may have come from, as well as what has happened to it since.

The not-so-obvious answer, as provided by ol' Henry Morris, is that most of this water existed in a sort of floating "canopy" of vapor which had been hanging over the earth (perhaps God had an inkling that He'd someday be inclined to drown everyone). Of course, there's no evidence that any such canopy ever existed, or that any such canopy is even possible – after all, the amount of water involved would be greater than that of every ocean, sea, lake, and rustic swimming hole on the planet. But this doesn't deter Henry Morris, as one might expect by this point – in fact, he even claims that such an allegedly possible canopy would have actually been of great value, as it would supposedly eliminate the effects of harmful radiations originating outside the planet. "It is known that these rays are harmful," declares Morris, "and are a chief cause of mutations and other deteriorative activity in living flesh." Here we go with the deterioration again. Actually, none of this is really "known" to anyone except Henry Morris himself, who has yet to provide evidence that these rays are truly harmful, or that an implausible vapor canopy would somehow deter them.

But vapor canopies aren't the only game in town; other creation scientists "hypothesize," in a loose sense of the term, that the water could have come from giant underground reservoirs. Of course, these reservoirs have yet to be detected, even by creation scientists, who could presumably just ask God real nice-like to point them in the proper direction.

As for how such water reserves could have been "pushed" out from below, another prominent creationist by the name of John Woodmorappe claims that "localized hyper-hurricanes" may have been used to pressure the water upwards. Good luck with all that, Johnny Boy.

And where did all this excess water eventually end up? Why, deep underground where we'll never find it, of course! This assertion opens up yet another can of worms, as the interior of the planet is actually known to be quite hot, and thus any water reserves which either originated or terminated so deep under the earth's surface would have boiled into steam.

Rainbows

After the flood had duly killed the estimated 235,000,000 people whom Henry Morris claims were around at the time, Yahweh is said to have reassured Noah's followers that "the waters shall no more become a flood to destroy all flesh," because in the future He plans on using giant pseudo-locusts to do His dirty work. And to show that He wasn't kidding, Yahweh then created a rainbow – the first rainbow in history, according to both the Bible and, more importantly, Henry Morris.

How's that again? No rainbows before the flood? As Morris tells it, the pre-flood climate had been mild and free of what we would recognize as rain, much less storms – constant, uniform weather patterns, he says, would have made both impossible, and thus the significance of this "first rainbow."

Perhaps Morris doesn't realize how much the absence of rain would complicate his narrative but he certainly doesn't seem to realize that rainbows can occur any time water droplets are hit by light at a low angle or altitude, and that waterfalls, water fountains, sprinkler systems, or something more mundane would easily suffice. Nor would water fountains or sprinkler systems be improbable according to creationist interpretations of the *Genesis* narrative – creation scientists posit a rather advanced civilization of the sort that would have allowed, say, eight people to build a giant ark which would not be matched in size until the latter 19th century. Ken Ham, in fact, thinks Noah may have built a circular saw. So why not a sprinkler system?

Hell, we can even work in those damned dinosaurs – certainly the urine stream of a brontosaurus would suffice for light refraction, particularly if the brontosaurus in question had been drinking plenty of water.

I'm sorry, but it had to be said.

The Ark

The search for Noah's Ark is one of those rare instances in which creation scientists have engaged in some semblance of actual field work. Of course, they've turned up nothing, but they're trying, damn it!

According to *Genesis*, the ark was quite a piece of craftsmanship: 438 feet long, 73 feet wide, and 34 feet high, and thus capable of displacing an estimated 19,940 tons of water, a feat which would not be achieved again until 1884. In fact, it could have been quite a bit larger than that, as the Hebrews used two measures known as a cubit, and the dimensions arrived at above are based on using the shorter version of the two, which the creation scientists have arbitrarily chosen in order to make their calculations slightly less ridiculous.

The "fact" that the ship was constructed with wood presents a few more problems. Wooden ships longer than 300 feet or so tend to warp and twist, while the hulls quickly take on water. The 329-foot, six-mast wooden ship *U.S.S. Wyoming*, for instance, was so unwieldy that it could only be sailed near the coast, as it leaked liked the dickens, was unsafe on rough seas, and was thus essentially useless, like the state for which it was named.

Then again, the U.S. Navy of the time didn't have access to "gopher wood," the mysterious material named in the Bible as the stuff that arks are made of. Though no one knows quite what gopher wood was, Ken Ham thinks he has an idea; the word "gopher," he's pointed out, sounds mildly similar to the Hebrew word "kaphar," which in turn means "atonement." Thus, gopher wood was actually magical, blessed-by-Yahweh wood, and thus we can presumably ignore all the impracticalities involved. Incidentally, in English, the name "Ham" means "ham," which is an unclean, unholy food that Yahweh forbade the Jews to have anything to do with. Just throwing that out there.

Not everyone is as quick to give up on the semblances

of science as Ken Ham is, though. The Bible states clearly that "pitch" was used to make the ark waterproof. But Henry Morris, who also believes that all such petroleum products as "pitch" are the result of the death brought on by the flood which had not yet occurred at the time of the ark's construction, believes that something else must have been used, because, after all, Henry Morris has already decided that pitch didn't exist yet. And thus Morris thinks that some other, yet-to-be-discovered substance must have been used. Hell, why not?

What about the construction of the ark itself? Was this improbably proportioned super-vessel really built by just eight people? If so, one wonders why the Pharaoh really needed thousands of Jews to build his pyramid when just a handful could have presumably done the job. But according to Ken Ham, Noah and his family had a few labor-saving methods at their disposal. For instance, they "could have easily used high speed circular saws and other labor saving, precision tools in the process of building the Ark." Let's not touch that one. Other creationists suppose he could have hired contractors (let's hope they spent the money before they drowned). And don't forget those dinosaurs. Ham again: "Can you imagine what a triceratops could do, with its giant tusks and protective bony crest over its head?" Yeah, Kenny. It could go extinct, like every other fucking dinosaur.

Animals

Perhaps the largest problem in this whole degenerate scenario is the one presented by the 30,000 or so animals and millions of insects which creationists believe were somehow herded onto the ark in a single day, apparently without any elephant-related bug crushings. Ken Ham, who apparently gives up easily, just falls back on miracles, which really makes you wonder why he even bothered to try to explain how Noah built the ark in the first place. At any rate, Yahweh used His Yahweh Powers to lead the whole mega-zoo onto the ark in an orderly fashion, and then caused the creatures in question to hibernate for much of the year-long voyage, whether they wanted to or not. This solves quite a few problems, like food, excretion, scorpion attacks, the need to exercise in order to avoid muscle entropy, and the fact that Ken Ham is an idiot.

But not everyone cops out so quickly. John Woodmorappe, for instance, once wrote a 306-page document in the style of a university-commissioned technical report called – seriously – "Noah's Ark: A Feasibility Study," in which he tries to explain the whole sordid affair without falling back on a single miracle. So, if you're ever looking for a good beach read, pick up a copy from your local...er...well, just order it from John Woodmorappe. You'll find out how eight people could take care of 16,000 animals with ten-hour workdays and six-day work weeks, which would certainly be news to the zoo keeper unions.

One sort of animal that Woodmorappe's over-worked Hebrews didn't have to contend with is the woolly mammoth, which many creationists agree didn't make it onto the ark for some reason or another. Instead, several of them managed to go and get themselves encased in ice, only to be found thousands of years later. This is a problem for creationists, since such deposits of ice are supposed to have not existed before the flood; even worse, we can tell from the preserved remains that the woolly mammoths were, well, woolly; if the Earth's climate was uniformly warm, breezy, and otherwise California-esque in its gentle perfection, it would hardly do for Yahweh to cover an elephant-type creature in a thick coat of hair – unless, of course, Yahweh is a spiteful prick, which can certainly be borne out by reading the *Book of Revelation*, the *Book of Job,* the *Book of Genesis*, the *Book of Exodus*, etc. At least, this would be a problem, if creationists gave a damn about consistency, which, incidentally, they do not.

But perhaps the greatest problem of all concerns what happens after the ark finally landed "on the mountains of Ararat" in present-day Turkey. Setting aside a hundred or so natural objections to the assertion that the 30,000 animals, millions of insects, and eight humans who then exited the ark were able to successfully establish themselves in a world in which all vegetation had been presumably destroyed by the flood, let's take a look at a couple of specific assertions of the creationist crowd.

How did all of these animals make it to their proper places afterwards (because now, you see, different climates suddenly existed, as they do today)? For instance, how did the penguins make it to the colder polar regions? How did the tree sloths manage to end up in Brazil? How did the armadillos make it to the sides of Texas highways? And why are there no armadillos in the Middle East, where they would have presumably started out, and where the climate and other factors would have suited them just fine? Everyone loves armadillos. If there's one thing the world needs, it's more armadillos. The little bastards are adorable. Hell, I'm gonna go find me an armadillo right now and give it a big hug.

What about marsupials, then? How did the great preponderance of them manage to get sequestered in Australia like so many Cockney thieves? Luckily, our old buddy John Woodmorappe explained this in one of his fine books, at least to the extent a creationist can ever be expected to explain anything. "It would have been no great difficulty for a post-Babel adventurer to have brought with him seventeen pairs of marsupial kinds from the Middle East to Australia," he explains, using the creationist word "kinds" instead of the grown-up word "species," and referring to the era after which Yahweh destroyed the Tower of Babel and told everyone to spread out a little bit and speak different languages. "Having a reminder of one's homeland is a powerful motivator for the introduction of animals... and, if some of the descendants of Noah's family had grown accustomed to marsupials near the respective homes in the Middle East area, they would thus have the motivation to take marsupials with them."

Apparently, they'd be motivated to take *all* the marsupials with them, and to be extra-super-careful that none of the little scamps managed to breed on the way to Australia. But one can easily imagine how one could get accustomed to marsupials in such an environment as the Middle East. Just think how cute they'd be, rolling over and dying because they didn't have access to eucalyptus leaves! *Awwwww!*

One might also wonder why a "post-Babel adventurer" became "accustomed" to marsupials and not something useful, like, say, horses, which are not native to Australia. Or what sort of sick asshole just up and leaves with every single marsupial, when other "post-Babel adventurers" would have presumably become "accustomed" to those marsupials as well.

"Sorry, guys, but I'm taking all the marsupials and headin' out of here."

"You suck, Isachiagigarelamish!"

"No, you suck!"

"Touche, old friend. You sure you don't want to take any of these horses, too?"

"Nah, they'd just get in the way."

At any rate, this wacky sort of process apparently went on all the time in the "post-Babel" world. Someone took all the penguin "kinds" to the polar regions, someone else took all of the Cape Buffalo "kinds" to Africa, while some poor, presumably masochistic fellow apparently decided to take most of the tree sloth and poisonous dart frog "kinds" to South America.

So, there you go. That's what people used to do.

Race

Ever wonder how a homogeneous family of only eight Hebrews managed to take on the wide variety of physical characteristics that we see in humanity today? Perhaps we should ask George McCready Price, whom you may recall as the father of creation science. McCready was once nice enough to express his opinion in more-or-less metered form:

> The poor little fellow who went to the south
> Got lost in the forests dank;
> His skin grew black, as the fierce sun beat
> And scorched his hair with its tropic heat,
> And his mind became a blank.

Aside from racism, McCready is also guilty of structural inadequacies, which is why his little poem sounds so horrid when read aloud. And surely we can't allow any such poetic expressions of racial derision stand unchallenged. Unfortunately, I'm writing this book from my private quarters at Augusta National, and thus there are no blacks around to answer McCready on their own behalf. So I'll just have to do it myself, while paying special attention to McCready's aforementioned affection for the Christ-appearance-predicting Seventh Day Adventist Church and its spiritual leader, William Miller:

> Poor Mr. McCready
> Was perhaps too damned speedy
> In deeming ol' Miller profound
> A hundred years after
> I'm stricken with laughter
> 'Cause Jesus has yet to be found.

A creationist might object that McCready wrote his ditty quite a long time ago, back in the days when even Frederick Douglas was a racist. And this is true. But what about modern creationists like Henry Morris?

"Sometimes the Hamites, especially the Negroes, have even become actual slaves to the others. Possessed of a genetic character concerned mainly with mundane, practical matters, they have often eventually been displaced by the intellectual and philosophical acumen of the Japhethites and the religious zeal of the Semites."

1976.

Not being an expert in Judeo-Christian pseudo-genetics, I'm not entirely sure who the Japhethites are supposed to be. Nonetheless, I feel another ditty coming on:

> That damned Henry Morris
> Was keen to inform us
> That the black man is lesser than he,
> Yet I can't help but notice
> That poor Henry Morris
> Is as dumb as a dumbass can be.

UFOs

As promised, here's a quick look at what certain key creation scientists think of the alleged UFO phenomenon – something that more orthodox scientists don't tend to dwell on. The skinny is duly provided by Kelly Segraves, author of several books on Noah's Ark, among other things. Let's just dive right in, shall we? From *Sons of God's Return*:

> "The Satanic entities posing as angels and ministers of light are deceiving people in these last days. In an attempt to destroy the pure and life-giving message of the Bible they have come as visitors from outer space."

Yipes. As comical as that may be, the next sentence is the real kicker:

> "But please remember, there is no scientific, empirical evidence for the existence of any being living outside our solar system."

Provide your own punch-line, because I refuse to shoot fish in a barrel with a shotgun, particularly when the fish are already dead. Besides, I'm on my break.

Segraves isn't just some minor character on the fringes of an otherwise serious-minded creationist movement, either. Aside from being a prolific author, he's also something of a folk hero to the anti-evolution crowd; back in 1981, he sued the State of California for teaching his kids the theory of evolution by way of its public school system (hey, he should just be happy they managed to teach them anything at all). Incidentally, he lost the case, which is why biology has yet to be replaced with *Demonic UFO Studies* in California public schools (or, if it has been, then it's for totally different reasons).

So, you know, creation science is kind of goofy, to say the least. But this is hardly the fault of the creation scientists themselves. In his book, *The Fossils Say No!* (see, they can't even refrain from putting exclamation marks in their book titles), creationist Duane Gish alludes to the difficulties that come with the territory. "We do not know how God created, what processes he used, for He used processes which are not now operating anywhere in the natural universe. This is why we refer to creation as special creation. We cannot discover by scientific investigations anything about the creative processes used by the creator." And that's a hell of a thing.

Not only did Yahweh refrain from making his processes clear, but He even went out of his way to muddy the waters. Unhappy with the well-established science of radiometric dating, which itself constitutes a death knell to any serious attempt to achieve scientific street cred for young-earth creationism, no less a Japhethite than Henry Morris himself has seriously proposed that Yahweh created such radioactive signatures in order to indicate that the Earth is far older than the 6,000 years alluded to by Biblical interpretations. After all, Morris says, if He could create Adam and Eve in their maturity, why not an entire universe as well?

Perhaps Morris is on to something here. Yahweh does indeed have a well-established tendency to test the faith of his followers, and discrediting the holy attempts of his most pious adherents to establish a young earth would certainly constitute the greatest test of all. And such trickery would also explain why Henry Morris and his son John are such disingenuous, pudding-brained goofballs; Yahweh could do nothing more to discredit the creationist movement by creating its most well-known proponents, if not in His own image, then in the image of some moderately retarded, would-be con artist.

Heck, I wouldn't put it past him.

FOUR

On Logos & Lesbianism

This is a fallen world. The good that God initially intended is no longer fully in evidence. Much has been perverted.

– William Dembski, *Intelligent Design: The Bridge Between Science and Theology*

Ask not why the old days were better; for that is a foolish question.

– Ecclesiastes 7:10

Let us now discuss Intelligent Design, starting from the beginning.

In the beginning, there was the *Logos*, a term meaning "word," derived from the Greeks and used by early Christians to indicate the Divine Word, or the mind of God made manifest. Just as the thoughts of a man take on discernible substance in the form of speech, the thoughts of God took on discernible reality in the form of the Logos. The mind of God called for there to be light, and thus the Logos brought about light, and light was. The mind of God called for there to be stars and planets; and oceans, and fish to dwell within them; and land, and animals to dwell upon it; and the Logos brought all these things about. The mind of God called for man to exist, and thus the Logos compels man to exist. The mind of God called for water to be composed of two hydrogen atoms and one oxygen atom, and thus the Logos compels it to be so. And for some reason or another, the mind of God also called for female bonobo chimpanzees to settle disputes by rubbing their respective vaginas together to the point of orgasm. And so the Logos caused this to be the case, possibly while giggling, assuming that the Logos is indeed capable of giggling, which it most likely is not.

"Wait just a damned second," you interject, rudely enough. "I thought we were going to discuss Intelligent Design, which is supposed to be a scientific concept. This sounds to me like Christian theology. Except for the part about bonobo vaginas. That's just kind of weird."

You are correct, Not-So-Gentle Reader. Intelligent Design is indeed supposed to be a scientific concept, in the same manner in which I'm supposed to be doing my laundry on a consistent basis. And just as I try to hide the fact that I'm wearing dirty underwear by spraying myself with Lysol, William Dembski and his buddies are attempting to hide the fact that they're wearing the Dirty Underwear of *A Priori* Religious Dogma by spraying themselves with the Lysol of Scientific Respectability. Now, my Lysol gambit will fool many people, just as Dembski's Lysol gambit will fool many people. But there will always be someone who sees through the ruse. In my case, it's my mother, who, like all mothers, has psychic powers. In Dembski's case, the ruse will be understood for what it is by any reasonable person who cares to examine Intelligent Design. The key difference between Dembski and myself, though, is that Dembski is a fool, whereas I am simply a fellow with dirty underwear. A certain bon mot attributed to Winston Churchill comes to mind.

But wouldn't it be goofy if I were to go to the trouble of spraying myself with Lysol, yet at the same time I decided to put a sign on my back that says, "I'm wearing dirty underwear"? The Reader will no doubt agree that this would be a goofy thing to do; it would, after all, make it possible for a person to immediately identify me as a wearer of dirty underwear, even without taking the trouble to smell me very carefully.

But Dembski and his brethren have essentially done just that. At the same time that they go to the trouble of spraying on their Lysol of Scientific Respectability, they also put on a sign indicating that they're actually wearing the Dirty Underwear of *A Priori* Religious Dogma. But they have a reason to do so – unlike literal dirty underwear, the Dirty Underwear of *A Priori* Religious Dogma is actually a popular garment among many of our fellow Americans. They call it "faith," and they wear it proudly. And by advertising the fact that they, too, wear this very same brand of dirty underwear, the Intelligent Design folks are thus able to signal to the faithful that both groups are fighting on the same side in the same war – The Crusade of the Dirty Underwear People.

My publisher has just informed me that I've been banned from using any further metaphors. This is probably for the best. But just so we're clear, what I'm getting at here is that the Lysol of Scientific Responsibility is the goofy manner in which Intelligent Design advocates claim that Intelligent Design is a purely scientific concept, the Dirty Underwear of *A Priori* Religious Dogma is the true purpose behind ID (Intelligent Design), and the sign that says "I'm wearing dirty underwear" is William Dembski's 1999 book, *Intelligent Design: The Bridge Between Science & Technology*," in which Dembski says things like, "Because God is the God of truth, the divine spoken word always reflects the divine *Logos*. At the same time, because the divine spoken word always constitutes a self-limitation, it can never comprehend the divine *Logos*." [Italics and idiocy in the original]

We're going to have a lot of fun going through Dembski's book, which should have been titled *A Smart Ass' Wet*

Dream or something like that. But that's not what it's called. It's called *Intelligent Design*, and it's full of Christian theology.

Now there's a good metaphor.

* * *

Before we find out what Intelligent Design really is, let's find out what it claims to be. First of all, it claims to be a scientific theory. That's fine, because I claim to be a nun. The U.S. National Academy of Sciences doesn't agree (with ID being a theory, that is; they have yet to weigh in on my nunhood); neither does the United States District Court for the Middle District of Pennsylvania, which ruled as much in the Dover trial (again, my case is still pending).

In science, a theory is not simply a wild guess, like when Bill Frist diagnoses someone. Instead, it's a collection of hypotheses which come together to describe a certain phenomenon. It can be used to make accurate predictions. It's useful. Its basic components have been peer-reviewed by qualified scientists. A good example would be the theory of evolution.

Unlike the theory of evolution, Intelligent Design is not a theory. Rather, it's a series of objections to the theory of evolution, none of which are really all that novel. A few appear to be deliberately obtuse. And all of them have been handily refuted many times over from a variety of different sources. On at least a few occasions, the relatively honest among them – by which I mean Michael Behe – have even accepted some of this criticism as at least partially valid.

Michael Behe, incidentally, may be considered to be one of Intelligent Design's more serious-minded proponents, insomuch as that he is capable of writing a book about Intelligent Design without making constant reference to the Logos and is also aware that man obviously evolved from lower species and that the Earth wasn't created a few weeks ago. This in itself is quite an accomplishment for an ID scholar, but Behe's true accomplishment in the field is his coinage of the term "irreducible complexity" to describe "a single system which is composed of several interacting parts that contribute to the basic function, and where the removal of any one of the parts causes the system to effectively cease functioning." According to Behe, the presence of an irreducibly complex system would constitute evidence that said biological systems were designed by an intelligent agent – let's say Loki – because, apparently, a system with several necessary, interacting parts simply cannot arise over millions of years of natural selection without Loki directing the whole process for his own undoubtedly double-edged ends.

As an example, let's say that biological System X requires elements Alpha, Beta, and Delta to properly perform its function, the function being to make fun of William Dembski (we're going to put the "fun" back in "function" here). Element Alpha is used to identify William Dembski. Element Beta is used to write down some sort of insult about whatever has caught its attention. Element Delta is used to make sure that the insult makes sense, and, if not, to rewrite it so that it does. Here we have an irreducibly complex system, because if one were to cause "the removal of any one of the parts," the system will "effectively cease functioning."

For instance, if we remove Element Alpha, System X is no longer capable of properly identifying William Dembski. Thus William Dembski walks by, humming to himself and thinking about how swell the Logos is, but System X doesn't have any way of differentiating William Dembski from some other William who also happens to be walking by – let's say it's William Bennett, former drug czar, noted moralist, and admitted gambler, overeater, and, c'mon, the guy obviously throws down a couple every now and then, at the very least. So System X, driven by Element Beta's compulsion to make fun of things, decides to insult William Bennett instead of William Dembski, not knowing the difference between the two. And because Element Delta is present, the insult is still going to make sense. The result:

> *"Hey, narc! How about you cool it with the blackjack and the bon-bons, you fat fuck?"*

Or, if we were to remove Element Beta, System X would still be capable of identifying William Dembski, and would also still be capable of making sure that any insult makes sense, but it would be incapable of writing down any insults in the first place. The result:

"..."

And if we were to instead remove Element Delta, System X would still be capable of identifying William Dembski, and of writing down an insult about whatever has been targeted, but the insult would be totally random, because System X would no longer be capable of making sure that the insult in question makes sense. The result:

> *"William Dembski, you're a finger cookie. I want to put you in my towel. Also, you smell of lavender. Poor William Dembski, the man from Sicily!"*

And William Dembski would be all like, "Huh?"

Now, an advocate of the irreducible complexity concept would tell you that, having observed the manner in which System X seems to become useless in the absence of any of its parts, we can thus determine that System X is irreducibly complex – it cannot logically have arisen out of natural selection, and must thus be the product of a designer (Loki). Of course, he would be wrong. System X could have indeed arisen out of natural selection, the complexity of System X notwithstanding.

Think of our little organism, which somehow derives

some sort of evolutionary benefit from giving William Dembski a hard time in general. The organism is the recipient of a mutation providing it with Element Beta, which, as you may recall, insults things. As people walk by the organism, Element Beta insults them. The insults don't necessarily make any sense, and they're just as likely to be directed towards William Bennett as they are to be towards William Dembski, who is really the only important target. Nonetheless, insults are being hurled at things, and so little energy is being expended in the course of the insult-hurtling that Element Beta is not really serving as much of a detriment to the organism. In fact, Element Beta actually ends up constituting a small net gain, because every once in a while, the insult sort of makes sense, simply by accident, and each time this occurs, there is a fifty percent chance of the insult being directed towards William Dembski and not William Bennett. So the organism, having successfully insulted William Dembski a couple of times, is now more likely to pass on his genes, including Element Beta, because, in our little hypothetical universe, being able to insult William Dembski gets the organism, like, book deals or something.

So our happy little organism has now produced some progeny, some of which are going to have this Element Beta gene. Each of these progeny, like its father before it, is slightly more capable of passing on its genes than the organisms around it. And thus, over time, Element Beta is going to be quite a popular gene among the organisms in our little organism population. Everybody who is anybody now has this gene.

Now, at some point, one of these lucky, Element Beta-possessing organisms is going to develop another mutation – Element Alpha, which identifies William Dembski. The organism is now twice as capable, on average, of insulting William Dembski, because there is no longer a fifty percent chance of any meaningful insults that develop being accidentally wasted on William Bennett. This organism is now quite a bit more likely than those around him to pass on his genes, and, being a virile fellow, our organism does so. Again, most of the resulting progeny now have both Element Alpha and Element Beta – two-thirds of our three-parted System X.

You know what's going to happen next. The organisms with Elements Alpha and Beta will come to dominate the population. And with so many organisms now possessing what has become a useful if imperfect system, it becomes more and more likely that, when Element Delta pops up out of a mutation, it will be popping up in an organism that can really make good use of it – an organism that is constantly hurling random insults at William Dembski. Element Delta ensures that the insults make sense, and the organism possessing all three elements has thus evolved System X, which will now flourish among the population to the point at which it is the rule, not the exception.

Of course, if we were to observe System X today and wonder how it came to be, we wouldn't know for sure how it developed. We would certainly suspect that Element Beta was developed first, but the development of Element Delta, and not Element Alpha, could have been the next step, to be followed then by Element Alpha. Or, if we were stupid, we would just give up and say that God made it.

In the real world, the sort of beneficial mutation process described above is augmented by all sorts of other important factors– errors in the process by which genes are combined during reproduction and which sometimes provide beneficial or at least neutral characteristics, the co-opting of pre-existing characteristics for new functions, gene duplication, the "brute force" successes that come with millions of years and trillions of organisms, and many other things. And the real world examples deemed to be irreducibly complex by Behe and others may be easily explained by such processes.

The bacterial flagellum, for instance, has become quite famous as of late, which is quite an achievement for any bacterial component. But the flagellum's real achievement is its complexity – utilizing several dozen protein components, this little motorized whip provides the bacteria with the ability to move around, acting as a sort of propeller. Incidentally, the flagellum derives its name from the Christian monastic practice of beating one's self with a whip, which is known as 'flagellating,' and which would be a very funny thing to see firsthand. No, no, I said flagellating.

Now, according to irreducible complexity buffs, the bacterial flagellum is a prime example of an irreducibly complex system. In his 1996 book *Darwin's Black Box*, which we'll mock briefly in the next chapter, Behe claims that if one were to remove any of the 40 or so protein components that seem to contribute to its operation, the system would cease to function and the flagellum would become useless. Thus, Behe claimed, we can safely assume that such a complex little system simply would not have evolved without guidance from Loki – after all, how could a complex system evolve if all the prior steps to its construction each resulted in a useless, perhaps even detrimental, result?

Unfortunately for Behe, the flagellum is quite a bit more capable than he originally supposed. For one thing, it was capable of turning around and biting Behe in the ass. Don't blame the flagellum for acting out, though; you'd be mad too, if someone was running around libeling you in the manner in which Behe libeled the flagellum.

Behe's assertions to the contrary, the flagellum is quite capable indeed of operating without each and every one of its protein components. In fact, about one third of the amino acids making up these proteins have been cut out of the system in a laboratory environment without any noticeable detriment to the motor function. And some flagella require fewer protein components to operate than others, while even the 40-protein flagella can lose several components without ceasing to function. Meanwhile, it's been discovered that much of the protein structure used for flagellum also exist in other bacteria – except that they serve completely different functions, unrelated to transportation. And so we can see how the flagellum, far from having been designed by Loki, could have easily evolved from previous, less complex structures, perhaps by way of the co-option of one pre-existing structure for an entirely different function.

Now, much of this exciting, flagellum-illuminating research wasn't conducted by scientists until *Darwin's Black Box* was already on the shelves. And therein lies the problem with irreducible complexity – like other "arguments from incredulity," IC can only flourish as a concept during the brief period extending from the time when something wondrous is discovered to the time when that wondrous something is better understood. In the case of flagellum, Behe thought he saw something that couldn't be properly explained through the naturalistic mechanism of natural selection. And he was right – for about a year.

* * *

William Dembski's *Intelligent Design: The Bridge Between Science and Theology* is a truly monumental work in the history of human thought. You can tell from all the fawning dust jacket blurbs.

For instance, University of Texas associate professor of philosophy Rob Koons made dust jacket history when he wrote that "William Dembski is the Isaac Newton of information theory, and since this is the Age of Information, that makes Dembski one of the most important thinkers of our time." He's certainly important to Koons, who describes himself on his UT website as "interested in deepening my philosophical understanding of the nature of God and our relationship to Him, and in exploring the correlations between philosophical insight and the One who is the Truth," presumably by randomly capitalizing things until they look all pretty.

And then you've got my personal favorite, provided by a fellow named Jack Collins:

"There are many things I admire about this book: its thoughtfulness, its philosophical and theological acumen, its willingness to face all difficulties. But the most important contribution is the effort to return the notion of design to its proper standing in science – that is, to bring science back under the rubric of rationality. Naturalism under the guise of science makes a lot of assumptions that it will now be forced to defend instead of assert."

So who is this Jack Collins fellow who seems to know so much about science and what ails it? Why, he's the professor of Old Testament studies at the Covenant Theological Seminary in St. Louis, Missouri! So, if you happen to be a scientist, take a steamboat down to St. Louis and look for Jack Collins. Maybe he'll give you some pointers.

But for sheer triumphalism, it's hard to top University of Texas Government and Philosophy professor J. Budziszewski:

"The toppling of the Berlin Wall will seem small in comparison with the impending demolition of scientific naturalism. Most of us have heard but a rumor of this event with our ears; Dembski is one of those making it happen."

Mr. Budziszewski is admittedly biased, though.

"As a philosopher of the natural moral law, I have particular reason to extol Dembski's work. There would be little point in speaking of a 'law written on the heart' if conscience were merely a meaningless byproduct of selfish genes."

God forbid that such an assuredly meaningful phrase as "law written on the heart" fall into disuse. And Budziszewski also has "particular reason" to throw the phrase around in the first place; it's a clever allusion to his own book, *Written on the Heart: The Case for Natural Law*, in which he no doubt explains why it is that "Natural Law" calls for lesbian orgies among bonobo chimpanzees, who are presumably acting under the dictates of "nature" and not liberal college professors or Angelina Jolie or some godless, supple-lipped combination of the two.

Incidentally, *Written on the Heart* is published by Inter-Varsity Press, which describes itself as a "publisher of books in Christian theology, Biblical studies, and cultural commentary," and which "serves those in the university, the church and the world by publishing resources that equip and encourage people to follow Jesus as Savior and Lord in all of Life." And InterVarsity Press, in turn, is simply the publishing arm of InterVarsity Christian Fellowship/USA, a "student movement active on campus at hundreds of universities, colleges and schools of nursing in the United States of America, and a member movement of the International Fellowship of Evangelical Students."

Not so incidentally, *Intelligent Design* is also published by InterVarsity.

Now, it would be hasty to suppose that this Evangelical "student movement" is not generally in the habit of publishing books on the subject of science. In fact, InterVarsity offers quite a few: *Science and Christianity: Four Views*, *Coming to Peace with Science* (that's reassuring), *The Creation Hypothesis*, *In Defense of Miracles*, and *Science & Its Limits*, among many others. See? The folks at InterVarsity really dig science. No wonder Dembski chose to publish with them. After all, Dembski digs science, too.

But Dembski digs science in the same manner in which an uptown girl digs the greaser mechanic from the wrong side of the tracks (sorry, Billy Joel's on the radio). Uptown Girl is quite taken with this strapping Greaser Mechanic; she likes his big muscles, his devil-may-care attitude, and, looking past all that, the sensitive side he conceals within. Maybe he has big dreams, like someday opening up his own garage. He's totally dreamy, you see. The bee's knees. Johnny Angel. Ooh, ah, ooh, ah, come on, Kitty, tell us about the boy from New York City.

Of course, it's always romantic when the well-bred broad in the poodle skirt takes a shine to the local bad boy:

> *"I met him at the candy store*
> *He turned around and smiled at me*
> *You get the picture?*
> *(Yes, we see!)*
> *And that's when I fell for*
> *The Leader of the Pack!*
> *(Vroom, vroom!)"*

Sweet, no? And her father disapproves, of course. 'That young punk is no damned good!' 'But, daddy, we're in love!' And then, at the end of the song, the greaser takes a spill on Dead Man's Curve, and then he's dead, thankfully enough.

That's the basic plot of "Leader of the Pack," anyway. But what about "Uptown Girl"? I have no idea, because I turned it off. It's actually kind of an irritating song. However, I think we can figure out what happens when all the obstacles to the relationship have finally been cleared, after that first blush of infatuation has finally run its course: Uptown Girl, having been disowned by Uptown Daddy, has now moved in with Greaser Mechanic. And Uptown Girl has come to realize that female adolescent fantasies aren't all that they're cracked up to be. First off, the two of them live in some crappy efficiency, and Greaser Mechanic cooks all their meals on a hotplate. He won't stop fiddling with that damned plastic black comb of his. And God forbid he cut down on the smoking. You know where he keeps his cigarettes? That's right, he keeps them rolled up in the sleeve of his white cotton t-shirt, like it's 1958 or something. Uptown Girl finds this very irritating, as well she might. And those uncouth friends of his! The boozy, gin-filled nights, when Greaser Mechanic comes home with other people's blood splattered all over his clothes! Uptown Girl needs a Miltown just thinking about it.

But Uptown Girl, don't you see the irony here? It was Greaser Mechanic's ultra-masculine charm that won your heart in the first place! And now you want to change him into something else, just because you come equipped with all your high-class baggage? This is who Greaser Mechanic is, baby, and he ain't changing for nobody!

Now, a similar situation exists between William Dembski and science. William Dembski met science in the candy store or what have you, and he was instantly infatuated with science's aura of respectability, its search for the truth, its incredible accomplishments. But just as Uptown Girl came equipped with all of her high-class baggage that she just couldn't get rid of, William Dembski came equipped with Jesus. And he wanted science to accept Jesus on Dembski's terms. He wanted science to abandon the very things that make science great in the first place. That aura of respectability, that search for truth, and those incredible accomplishments weren't just handed to science on a silver platter – science took on these characteristics by way of its dedication to methodological naturalism. But methodological naturalism doesn't leave much room for Jesus. And Jesus makes William Dembski feel good about himself.

Dembski just couldn't take it. A nasty breakup followed. Things were said. Hotplates were broken. And the worst part, for Dembski, was that science never really gave a damn about him in the first place. This breaks Dembski's heart. And thus, like a crazy ex-girlfriend, Dembski is now running around bad-mouthing science.

Unfortunately, science can't get a restraining order or anything like that.

***

"Naturalism is the disease," Dembski writes. "Intelligent Design is the cure."

Dembski has little regard for naturalism. Or for naturalists:

> "Those who are blind to God's action in the world have one overriding satisfaction: That this world belongs to them and to them alone. Call those who are blind to God's action in this world 'naturalists,' and call the view that nature is self-contained 'naturalism.'"

Okay, done. So what's the problem with naturalism, anyway?

"Naturalism leads irresistibly to idolatry."

Holy shit. But Dembski doesn't mean to imply that scientists are sacrificing lambs to their microscopes or anything weird like that:

> "Idolatry is not so much a matter of investing any particular object with extraordinary significance. Rather it is a matter of investing the world with a significance it does not deserve."

Which is to say, naturalism leads to naturalism. Hey, he's right! But seriously, idolatry is terrible stuff:

> "The severing of the world from God is the essence of idolatry and is in the end always what keeps us from knowing God. Severing the world from God, or alternatively viewing the world as nature, is the essence of humanity's fall."

And you probably didn't even realize that humanity had fallen. Well, it has. William Dembski just said so. And William Dembski is the Isaac Newton of information theory, for Christ's sake! Literally, I mean; he does it for the sake of Christ.

But you know what really bugs Dembski about naturalism? All of the *a priori* assumptions entailed therein. "In fact, science provides no evidence for naturalism one way or the other, though the assumption of naturalism profoundly affects how we do science." For instance, naturalism just assumes that we don't know for a scientific fact that "Christ is also the incarnate Word who through the incarnation enters and transforms the whole of reality," as Dembski is nice enough to tell us. And whereas Dembski realizes that "the validity of the scientist's insights can never be divorced from Christ, who through the incarnation enters, takes on and transforms the world and thus cannot help but pervade the scientist's domain of inquiry," naturalism is so foolish as to simply assume that this might not necessarily be the case.

"The Bible uses many words and images to characterize idolatry," notes Dembski, "but the most apt is foolishness. What can be more foolish than to elevate what is second best to what is best? It's like preferring the publisher of Shakespeare to Shakespeare himself. It's like preferring golden eggs to the goose that lays the golden eggs." It's like when a Christian who despises naturalism wears glasses to correct his vision instead of just praying to Jesus for a miracle. Incidentally, Dembski wears glasses.

On the other hand, we have the theists. "Theists know that naturalism is false. Nature is not self-sufficient." Finally, some cold, hard facts! Forsooth!

Where did all of this darned naturalism come from, anyway? Dembski traces the problem back to the 19th century, when British natural theology took a back seat to the theory of evolution. In fact, the third chapter of *Intelligent Design* is entitled "The Demise of British Natural Theology." If the term

"British natural theology" is unfamiliar to you, this may be because no one gives a shit about British natural theology, for the same reason that no one gives a shit about Voodoo. British natural theology produced absolutely nothing, most likely because British natural theology was not science, but rather theology, and not even original theology at that. Whereas the theory of evolution went on to prove its veracity by developing into an integrating force among the fields of biology, genetics, anatomy, biochemistry, paleontology, and plenty else besides, British natural theology was a parlor game in which all the players immediately conceded and then spent the rest of the evening discussing why it was that they lost. It was a surrender to mystery followed by commentary, indistinguishable from a dozen pre-scientific surrenders that came before it.

For instance, there was Cicero, who noted that if one were to come across a clock on the beach, one would naturally assume that the clock had been the product of design, not chance, and that it follows that the universe itself is the product of design, even though that doesn't really follow at all. Two thousand years later, you have William Paley, whom William Dembski describes as "the prince of British natural theologians," and who is best known for the following observation:

> "In crossing a heath, suppose I pitched my foot against a stone, and were asked how the stone came to be there; I might possibly answer, that, for anything I knew to the contrary, it had lain there forever: nor would it perhaps be very easy to show the absurdity of this answer. But suppose I had found a watch upon the ground, and it should be inquired how the watch happened to be in that place; I should hardly think of the answer I had before given, that for anything I knew, the watch might have always been there...
> There must have existed, at some time, and at

> some place or other, an artificer or artificers, who formed it for the purpose which we find it actually to answer; who comprehended its construction, and designed its use...Every indication of contrivance, every manifestation of design, which existed in the watch, exists in the works of nature; with the difference, on the side of nature, of being greater or more, and that in a degree which exceeds all computation."

Which is to say, if there is a clock, there must be a clockmaker. After all, you've seen a clock before. You know from experience that clocks generally derive from the design of intelligent entities. You know how a clock works. And clocks serve a definite purpose. Thus, this makes for a swell universal maxim when one finds a clock while crossing a heath, a bog, or even a shire.

Unfortunately for the analogy itself, none of these fundamental characteristics actually apply to the universe. After all, you've never seen a universe before. You don't know from experience that universes generally derive from the design of intelligent entities. You don't know how the universe works. And the universe doesn't seem to serve a definite purpose. In fact, you might even go so far as to call the whole thing a bad analogy, and I should talk, what with all that Uptown Girl nonsense.

Speaking of bad analogies, Dembski has the following to say about his favorite philosophy's ultimate place in the history books:

> "Contemporary accounts of British natural theology almost invariably treat natural theology as a foil to Darwin's theory of evolution. Thus natural theology becomes the evil stepchild that from time immemorial has defiled her noble

sister biology."

Isn't that horrible? What the hell does that mean? Because it sounds horrible. But you understand what Dembski is getting at; British natural theology has been unfairly relegated to the history books, when it more properly belongs in the textbooks. As things stand now, if one looks up the phrase "British natural theology" on Yahoo or Google or Chitty Chitty Bang Bang or whatever, most of the results are links to articles by William Dembski talking about how nifty British natural theology is, and most of the rest are links to articles by creationists talking about how nifty William Dembski is.

But as annoying as it might be to literal-minded Christians, the inevitable victory of Darwinism over stupid analogies isn't even Dembski's central complaint; rather, the decline of British natural theology is emblematic of a larger, more profound paradigm shift, one that Dembski rightly identifies as an obstacle to Christian literalism: modernity.

You see, "Jesus urges his followers to accept the test-conditional If I resurrect, then I've mastered death and so will you. Accepting this test-conditional requires faith." But the presence of faith doesn't mean the absence of scientific rigor: "At the same time, accepting this test-conditional does not require a 'leap of faith' – this is not a matter of arbitrary or unexamined acceptance. Jesus' resurrection was fully observable." And that's why, today, everyone believes that Jesus was resurrected, and members of "Jews for Jesus" are welcomed into Brooklyn with open arms.

Seriously, what does Dembski mean when he states, as fact, that "Jesus' resurrection was fully observable"? It certainly wasn't fully observed. Open up your Bible, or, if you don't have one, mug a Gideon. Turn to the end of the *Book of Matthew*. Read it. Now, do the same thing with the *Book of Mark*, the *Book of Luke*, and the *Book of John*. Notice how each of these texts claim that no one actually saw any resurrections occur.

But try to refrain from reading each book very carefully and noticing that they all contradict each other in other places. Be doubly sure not to do any research into the origins of the New Testament, and take particular care not to learn anything about the Byzantine Empire, the Council of Nicaea, Constantine and that bitch stepmother of his, or, most especially, all of the earlier religious traditions from which Christian mythology has obviously stolen from, and rather liberally at that. After all, these are the sorts of things that a "modernist" might do.

The modernist's unholy addiction to empirical evidence blinds him to things that are self-evident to William Dembski, Jerry Falwell, and people who think that Uri Geller has psychic powers. Thus, the modernist is scornful of what Dembski calls "pre-modernity" and what reasonable people refer to as "the Dark Ages."

"Typically pre-modernity is identified with superstition, astrology, witchcraft, witch trials, alchemy, Ptolemaic epicycles, the four humors, the four elements and so on – what C.S. Lewis called the 'discarded image,'" Dembski asserts, correctly enough. "Now there is no question that many elements of premodernity needed to be discarded. Nonetheless, premodernity had had one thing going for it that neither modernity nor postmodernity could match, namely, a worldview rich enough to accommodate divine agency."

Not to mention superstition, astrology, witchcraft, witch trials, alchemy, Ptolemaic epicycles, the four humors, the four elements, and so on. And it's funny that Dembski should mention witchcraft; a 2004 Opinion Dynamics poll showed that a quarter of Americans still believe in witches. Now, how many of that quarter do you suppose are "modernists"? By definition, zero. On the other hand, how many do you suppose are evangelical Christians?

Dembski doesn't explain how it is that he has managed to rule out the existence of witches without falling back on "modernist" thinking. This is probably for the best, as many of the sort of people who end up doing the groundwork in the Intelligent Design movement really do believe in witches. Remember InterVarsity, the evangelical publisher that brought out Dembski's book? Along with *Intelligent Design*, they also offer a fantastic volume called *Powers of Darkness*. Here's the description from the InterVarsity website:

> *"Satan worship. Witches. New Age channelers.*
> *The last two decades have witnessed a vast upsurge in occult activity. Scores of popular books have warned Christians of the dangers and urged them to do battle against these spiritual forces. Few books, however, have developed a careful biblical theology on demons, principalities and powers.*
> *Clinton Arnold seeks to fill this gap, providing an in-depth look at Paul's letters and what they teach on the subject. For perspective, he examines first-century Greek, Roman and Jewish beliefs as well as Jesus' teaching about magic, sorcery and divination. Arguing against many recent interpretations that have seen principalities and powers as impoersonal [sic] social, economic and political structures, Arnold contends that the New Testament view is that such forces are organized, personal beings which Jesus defeated at the cross and whill [sic] bring into full subjection at his return."*

> In his concluding section Arnold suggests practical ways in which Christians today can contend with the forces of evil.
> *"A thoughtful, biblical look at an urgent challenge facing the church."*

This actually sounds like a pretty interesting book. It would be particularly illuminating to find out about the "practical ways in which Christians today can contend with the forces of evil." Who wants to bet that "helping the poor" takes a back seat to "forcing exorcisms on the mentally ill" or "ringing doorbells for Sam Brownback"? And how long before the nation's evangelicals start clamoring for public schools to teach sixth graders about the dangers of demonic divination? They've got to replace sex ed with something.

At any rate, Dembski has apparently figured out some method of differentiating between the sort of pre-modern thinking that "needed to be discarded" and the sort of pre-modern thinking that helps him feel better about himself. And thus we need no longer fear the mistakes of the past, as Dembski reminds us:

> "Johannes Kepler, for instance, thought the craters on the moon were intelligently designed by moon dwellers. We now know that the craters were formed naturally. It's this fear of falsely attributing something to design only to have it overturned later that has prevented design from entering science proper. With precise methods for discriminating intelligently from unintelligently caused objects, scientists are now able to avoid Kepler's mistake."

Except for when they aren't, like when Michael Behe decided that God must have built the flagellum. Remember that? Well, Dembski does, although his memory is understandably selective. In fact, he actually points to Behe's work as evidence that "there does in fact exist a rigorous criterion for distinguishing intelligently caused objects from unintelligently caused ones." And, of course, Behe's assertions have since turned out to be demonstrably incorrect. Incidentally, the foreword to *Intelligent Design* is written by one Michael Behe.

"Who's right, the ancients or the moderns?" Dembski asks, apparently rhetorically. "My view is that the ancients got it right."

But Dembski can't build a time machine and go live in

the ancient world, with its "worldview rich enough to accommodate divine agency," such as the belief that lightning bolts indicate that Zeus is upset about something. Instead, he's forced to exist in unhappy modernity, in a world in which the "premodern logic of signs," as he calls it, is publicly trumped by the modern logic of not being a dunderhead. That's right; I called him a dunderhead. I'm assuming that it's some sort of insult. If not, I take it back.

Dembski does have one method of recourse, though. The ways of the ancients could be restored. "My aim in this book then is to take this premodern logic of signs and make it rigorous," Dembski notes early on. "In doing so, I intend to preserve the valid insights of modern science as well as the core commitments of the Christian faith." Especially the belief in the Logos. After all, as Dembski wrote in the Christian magazine *Touchstone* in 1999, "Intelligent Design is just the Logos theology of John's Gospel restated in the idiom of information theory."

Oh. Well, in that case, we'd better learn a thing or two about the Logos.

When we last left the Logos, it was commanding bonobo chimpanzees to engage in various unorthodox sexual habits. And although this command is not specifically addressed by the apostle John, from whom we're apparently getting all of our scientific concepts nowadays, we may nonetheless assume this to be the case; after all, from the standpoint of the modern literalist Christian, all of God's creations were created by Him, under the auspices of the Logos, just a few thousand years ago, and have remained more or less the same in the years since.

If one wishes to annoy a literalist Christian, the first thing to do is to ask him where all of the bonobo orgies fit in to God's divine plan. The literalist Christian will have an answer, of course, or perhaps even several. For instance, he could go the Henry Morris route and point to the "degeneracy" of species (or "kinds") brought on by the Fall. He could somehow blame Satan, whom certain Christians believe to be in the habit of corrupting children and ruining credit ratings, and who thus presumably wouldn't be above teaching bonobos all sorts of horrible, pleasurable things. But whatever the response, the literalist Christian is in no way obligated to concede that God himself may have ordained such behavior, because he has never committed God to having directly intervened in the creation of any behavior that the literalist Christian finds objectionable.

But William Dembski has, as we shall soon see. By linking certain aspects of the natural world to God so directly, Dembski has forced his deity into evidential complicity with some of the natural world's less desirable characteristics. To his credit, Dembski sees this trap and makes an effort to avoid it, but in the end, he cannot, because the trap is unavoidable due to the silly parameters that Dembski has himself concocted. Think of it as theological splash-back. Better yet, think up a cleverer term and then think of it as that. First, though, I've got to tell you how it was that Dembski managed to accidentally slander his favorite Mediterranean deity.

* * *

"Nature is responsible for the giraffe's neck, the eagle's talons and the angler fish's lure," Dembski tells us. Now, these are all more or less benevolent things, unless one happens to be prey for the giraffe, the eagle, or the angler fish. But nature is also responsible for things which, beyond serving the arguably benevolent purpose of allowing God's creations to feed themselves, also appear needlessly cruel to modern eyes. One of the more oft-mentioned examples of these was actually made famous by Darwin himself, who once responded to a religious critic thusly:

> "But I own that I cannot see as plainly as others do, and as I should wish to do, evidence of design and beneficence on all sides of us. There

seems to me too much misery in the world. I cannot persuade myself that a beneficent and omnipotent God would have designedly (apparently that's actually a word) created the Ichneumonidae with the express intention of their feeding within the living bodies of caterpillars, or that a cat should play with mice."

Darwin is referring to what is today known as the ichneumon, a wasp which deposits its larvae into the body of a host – often a caterpillar, as Darwin notes – so that these larvae can later hatch and devour the host, starting with the least essential organs and ending with the most essential in order that the organism may remain alive long enough to serve as an adequate, never-ending buffet for the larvae in question.

Rather evil-sounding indeed. And, worse yet, some of Dembski's critics have pointed to such rather complex manifestations of evil as a potential thorn in the side of Intelligent Design. Is the methodology of the ichneumon an instance of design? If so, does this mean that God purposely designs evil mechanisms?

Dembski denies it, and notes that "critics who invoke the problem of evil against design have left science behind and entered the waters of philosophy and theology," as if one has any choice when dealing with Dembski, who has spent most of his book advocating the messy convergence of all three of these things. Nonetheless, Dembski has an answer.

"This is a fallen world," he tells us. "The good that God initially intended is no longer fully in evidence. Much has been perverted." Dembski goes on to explain that when we see any such "perverted" aspects of nature, what we are seeing is simply an instance of "perceived design" – something which appears designed at first glance, but which is actually not designed at all. "Perceived design," you see, does not actually involve "specified complexity," and only "specified complexity," such as the sort we allegedly see in the flagellum, is a true hallmark of God's design. "Perceived design," on the other hand, is, like most things, the result of "mutation and natural selection," a process that Dembski does acknowledge, at least to some extent. He reminds us that "the design theorist is not committed to every biological structure being designed." The problem, Dembski states, is that "objects intended for good purposes are regularly co-opted and used for evil purposes."

Do you notice anything surreal about that last statement? Change the adjectives to something neutral, and you have the following statement:

"Objects intended for some purposes are regularly co-opted and used for other purposes."

This is the exact argument that evolutionists use in arguing against Intelligent Design.

You see what's happened here. Dembski's love of theology overrides his love of science. When one points out aspects of nature that threaten to disrupt his theology, Dembski suddenly taps into that part of his mind that he otherwise leaves intentionally closed off – which is to say, his scientific imagination. Point to the ichneumon, and Dembski is suddenly capable of seeing how complex behavior can arise from natural selection. Suddenly, processes wondrous in their specificity and their complexity just don't meet the criteria for "specified complexity."

But Dembski would be okay on this point, assuming that he can demonstrate how all of nature's lovable complexity is "specified complexity," whereas all of nature's less desirable complexity is not. The problem is that Dembski has already provided us with examples of what constitute specified complexity, many of which are neither specified nor complex. More importantly, though, some of his benevolent examples are less "specified" and less "complex" than the evil ones that we can point to.

For instance, if the flagellum is an example of specified

complexity, certainly the ichneumon is as well. Can Dembski object? Can Dembski show us how such specified, complex, evil behavior arose through "mutation and natural selection," as he indicates that it did? Can he trace the evolutionary path of this particular system? Can he give us the exact intermediate steps that led to such complexity? If not, does that mean that there are "gaps" in the theological components of Intelligent Design? Is Dembski depending too much on naturalism? Is he blind to God's malevolent hand in the world? Has he no sense of premodernity? Has he no "worldview rich enough to account for divine agency?" Why does he assume that the ichneumon arose naturally, as opposed to having been expressly designed by a God who hates caterpillars and wants them dispatched in as viscous a manner as possible? And what about the ants who enslave aphids in order to "milk" them? And those which enslave other ants? And what about the organized, militaristic genocidal practices of ants in general? When will Dembski show us how all of these arose out of natural selection?

Dembski and his cohorts have been leveling these sorts of inane questions at evolutionists for 150 years now. Most likely, they never considered that they might someday be forced into a position in which they'd have to answer these very same questions, using some of the same answers that the evolutionists themselves have provided for them in advance. And if they find such questions to be difficult, they have nobody to blame but the leaders of the Intelligent Design movement, who sought a "Bridge Between Science and Theology" while not being all that proficient at either.

Such a situation is a new one for creationists in particular, but an old one for faith-based institutions in general. The problem, I think, is imagination – lacking in matters of science, and overflowing in matters of theology.

Kind of like pre-modernity.

FIVE

Constantine vs. The Enlightenment

I have recently been examining all the known superstitions of the world, and do not find in our particular superstition one redeeming feature. They are all alike, founded upon fables and mythologies.

– Thomas Jefferson

Religious controversies are always productive of more acrimony and irreconcilable hatreds than those which spring from any other cause. I had hoped that liberal and enlightened thought would have reconciled the Christians so that their religious fights would not endanger the peace of Society.

– George Washington

How has it happened that millions of myths, fables, legends and tales have been blended with Jewish and Christian fables and myths and have made them the most bloody religion that has ever existed? Filled with the sordid and detestable purposes of superstition and fraud?

– John Adams

Some volumes against deism fell into my hands. They were said to be the substance of sermons preached at Boyle's Lecture. It happened that they produced on me an effect precisely the reverse of what was intended by the writers; for the arguments of the Deists, which were cited in order to be refuted, appealed to me much more forcibly than the refutation itself. In a word, I soon became a thorough Deist.

– Benjamin Franklin

All national institutions of churches, whether Jewish, Christian or Turkish, appear to me no other than human inventions, set up to terrify and enslave mankind, and monopolize power and profit.

– Thomas Paine

There are in this country, as in all others, a certain proportion of restless and turbulent spirits – poor, unoccupied, ambitious – who must always have something to quarrel about with their neighbors. These people are the authors of religious revivals.

– John Quincy Adams

My earlier views of the unsoundness of the

Christian scheme of salvation and the human origin of the scriptures have become clearer and stronger with advancing years and I see no reason for thinking I shall ever change them.

– Abraham Lincoln

This country was founded on Christianity, and our students should be taught as such.

– William Buckingham

There are two basic schools of thought regarding what it means to be an American. The first holds that the United States is a product of the Enlightenment, and ought to be governed in accordance with the precepts of that particular movement. The second holds that the United States is a product of Christianity, and ought to be governed in accordance with the precepts of that particular movement. The first school of thought tends to dwell on the Bill of Rights; the second tends to dwell on the Ten Commandments, at least until it becomes inconvenient to do so.

The question of what the Founding Fathers intended is debatable, if only in the sense in which everything is debatable, which is to say that, like many other things, it is often the subject of debate. But there is no legitimate debate to be had, as the Founding Fathers have already weighed in, and they would certainly know. Also weighing in on the issue are Abraham Lincoln and John Quincy Adams. That's right. John Quincy Adams.

Now, this is not to say that one cannot found a nation on Christianity. After all, it's been done before. The Byzantine Empire, for instance, was the first major political entity to be created by Christians, for Christians, and in general accordance with Christian theology, incomplete as it was at the time.

Gaius Flavius Valerius Aurelius Constantinus, later to be known simply as Constantine, was a very pre-modern fellow, and a lucky one at that. Unlike our modernistic naturalists of the present day, Constantine understood the "pre-modern logic of signs," as William Dembski likes to call it. And for this faith, he was well rewarded. According to none other than Constantine himself, the royal-blooded go-getter was once favored with a meeting with the sun god Apollo, who appeared to Constantine one fine day in order to tell him what a swell fellow he was.

Now, Constantine wasn't the sort of humbug who would keep something as wonderful as this to himself; on the contrary, he made a point of telling everyone who would listen, and even commemorated the event for posterity by issuing coins depicting himself with his buddy Apollo, building statues of himself in which he kind of looked like Apollo, and occasionally sort-of-kind-of implying that he himself actually was Apollo, or at least a fantastic manifestation thereof.

Now, this divinely ordained meeting with Apollo was quite fortunate, as Constantine was at the time embroiled in a struggle for supremacy over the Roman Empire with his brother-in-law Maxentius, and thus could use all the favor-of-the-gods street cred he could get. Whereas Constantine was merely Caesar, and thus had to make do with ruling only Britannia and Gaul, Maxentius was emperor of what we now call the Western Roman Empire. Constantine didn't care for this one bit; nor did Apollo, we may presume, since he had already thrown his hat in with Constantine.

In the summer of 312, Maxentius and Constantine were able to come to what was at the time considered a reasonable solution to their dispute – the two would both assemble their respective legions, meet outside of Rome, and then attempt to kill each other. Constantine failed to bring enough boppers to the rumble though, and thus his forces were vastly outnumbered by those of Maxentius. But Constantine, being a veritable deity magnet, once again attracted divine attention.

As he would later tell his admirers, Constantine was just minding his own business, praying to his pagan gods for victory before the battle, when he happened to glance at the sun, which he was in the habit of worshiping at the time. But then, something unusual happened. Superimposed upon the sun was a cross; and upon the ears of blessed Constantine fell the words, "In Hic Signo Vinces," which roughly translates to "Use the Force, Luke" but less roughly translates to "In this sign you will conquer." Inspired and apparently literal-minded, Constantine commanded his soldiers to paint crosses on their shields. And then, of course, they won the battle. After all, they had painted crosses on their shields.

(Incidentally, hundreds of years later, Christian combatants were still painting crosses on their shields when fighting other Christians who had painted crosses on their shields, and suddenly the ol' paint-a-cross-on-your-shield trick now only seemed to work half of the time.)

Constantine eventually converted to Christianity, which was certainly swell for Christianity, as Constantine soon became emperor of a reunified Roman Empire. Suddenly, Christianity was the new black, and it soon occurred to various court eunuchs, upwardly mobile wives, and other fashionable types that they now believed in Jesus. The problem was that nobody was quite sure exactly what it was that they were supposed to believe about Jesus, as there were still several competing theologies in the running. This led to occasional outbreaks of violence and, worse, heresy. One of the most prominent of these various concoctions, Arianism, taught that the Father had created the Son, and was thus older than the Son and perhaps superior to him as well. Luckily, the state was on hand to settle the matter, and after a series of imperially enforced theological resolutions, it eventually became clear that, in fact, God consisted of the Father, the Son, and the Holy Spirit, each of which was an equal and eternal component of the greater deity. And it became equally clear that to believe otherwise was now illegal.

But despite the obvious dedication on the part of Constantine and his successors towards molding the nascent Byzantine Empire into a distinctly Christian enterprise, they seemed to have overlooked a few details. After all, if the democratic ideals of the United States are derived from the application of the Christian religion, it would seem to follow that the application of the Christian religion would tend to lead to the democratic ideals of the United States. Oddly enough though, this didn't seem to be the case among the Byzantines. The Reader will notice, for instance, that Constantine forgot to hold a national election to choose his successor, who himself would in turn be obliged to seek re-election after another four years. Other things that appear to have slipped Constantine's mind include establishing a bicameral legislature and an independent judiciary, guaranteeing freedom of speech and of religious expression, and providing for limits on government power. In fact, one might go so far as to say that he did the opposite of all of these things, which is why transfer of executive power was a bit more spirited in the Byzantine world than it generally is in the United States.

For instance, Emperor Basilicus starved to death in prison. Zeno was buried alive. Maurice, Leontius, Tiberius III, and Justinian II had their heads removed from their bodies by way of various sharp objects. Phocas was simply dismembered. Heracleonas was mutilated. Constantine III, Constantine VII, Romanus II, and John I were poisoned. Constans II was bludgeoned to death in his own bathtub. Constantine VI, Philippucus, Michael V, Isaac II, John IV, Andronicus IV, and John VII were blinded. Alexius IV was strangled. Leo V and Nicephorus II were both stabbed and decapitated. Romanus III was poisoned and drowned, presumably in that order. Romanus IV was poisoned and blinded. Alexius II was both strangled and decapitated (you can never be too sure). Andronicus I was mutilated and tortured. Alexius V was blinded and maimed. Altogether, 29 Byzantine emperors ended up relinquishing power as a result of being blinded, poisoned, drowned, tortured, starved, maimed, bludgeoned, strangled, decapitated, or some combination thereof, generally by other Christians who really, really wanted to be

Emperor. And each time this happened, it was widely presumed that the victor had succeeded because God had wanted him to succeed. The Byzantines were people of faith.

Now, there's a very simple reason for all of this Byzantine malarkey: Christianity in and of itself does not lead to democracy. Christianity in and of itself has never lead to democracy, which is why, in the first 1500 years of Christianity's history, no democracy ever arose in the Christian world. And why would it? Nothing at all that could possibly be interpreted as anything approaching an endorsement of modern democratic ideals can be found in what is today called the New Testament. Nor will you find a *Republic* of Israel in the Old Testament, nor even a *People's Republic* of Israel, with its myriad kibbutzim and collectivized delis. But you will indeed find a *Kingdom* of Israel, as well as instructions regarding how badly one may beat one's slaves without facing punishment (the answer, by the way, is very badly).

It was not until the 19th century, in the wake of the Enlightenment, that a small contingent of mostly non-Christian political leaders broke off from a Christian monarchy in order to establish the world's first modern constitutional republic, which, coincidentally enough, would also operate under the first officially non-religious governmental framework in the recorded history of mankind.

Aside from the First Amendment, the stated positions of our most prominent Founding Fathers, and common sense (not to mention *Common Sense*), the non-aligned nature of the United States government was spelled out very specifically in the Treaty of Tripoli, which was ratified by the Senate in 1797, signed by President John Adams and Secretary of State Timothy Pickering, and which included the following declaration:

> As the Government of the United States of America is not, in any sense, founded on the Christian religion; as it has in itself no charac-

ter of enmity against the laws, religion, or tran-
quility, of Mussulmen; and, as the said States
never entered into any war, or act of hostility
against any Mahometan nation, it is declared
by the parties, that no pretext arising from religious opinions, shall ever produce an interrup-
tion of the harmony existing between the two
countries.

Incidentally, Tripoli is now the capitol of Libya.
Teehee.

But the Founding Fathers are dead, and half of America
is largely ignorant. A 2005 Gallup poll indicated that 53 percent
of American adults believe that "God created humans in their
present form exactly the way the Bible describes it." But things
aren't quite as bleak as they seem. The minority of Americans
who ascribe to non-supernatural evolution – thirteen percent,
according to that Gallup poll – happen to be distributed in such a
way that they can prevent a religiously-motivated pseudoscience
like Intelligent Design from getting the free pass that its advocates have been demanding. For instance, that thirteen percent
happens to make up the vast majority of American scientists, as
well as a ridiculously vast majority of biologists. Perhaps this is
just a coincidence. More likely, it's a "sign."

* * *

Intelligent Design was never meant to win in the scientific sphere, at least not before the scientific sphere has been
brought to its knees by the Great Unwashed; a theological mon-
strosity "supported" by William Dembski's adolescent word
games and "backed up" by Michael Behe's easily-refuted arguments from ignorance, cannot prosper in the current scientific
framework, which has a tendency to make inconvenient de-

mands upon those who would call themselves scientists. And to their credit, the key backers of the Intelligent Design movement are aware of all this. And thus their strategy hinges not on unassailable scientific research or useful new theories or anything of that nature, but rather on an unprecedented public relations offensive aimed at capturing the imagination of a scientifically illiterate voting public, which may then be depended upon to provide Intelligent Design with the logistical support it needs to prevail over real science. Rather than a new and exciting theory, the Intelligent Design movement is nothing less than an attempted coup by which a contingent of Constantines hopes to overthrow the legacy of the Enlightenment.

If this sounds like hyperbole, the Reader need not take my word for it, as this very strategy has been spelled out quite plainly by the leaders of the Intelligent Design movement. It has even been given a name; they call it "the Wedge Strategy." And under the auspices of its Center for the Renewal of Science & Culture, the Discovery Institute released this strategy to sympathetic financial backers several years ago, while never making it available to the general public. Luckily, the document was stolen from the Discovery Institute's Seattle-area headquarters shortly after it was written, and may now be read by anyone who cares to know the true nature of the Intelligent Design movement.

The Discovery Institute does not dispute that this document is real. In fact, they've released at least one article defending it (if you'd care to hear them out, the article may be found on the Discovery Institute website, and is entitled, with characteristic charm, "So What?"). And where portions of the document have been cited by opponents as evidence that the Discovery Institute is merely a propaganda outfit, the Discovery Institute has countered by claiming that such portions have been "taken out of context."

Well, we wouldn't want to take anything out of context; that's a practice better left to the professionals at the Discovery Institute, as you'll see later in the chapter. And thus, for the Reader's edification and potential beach-reading pleasure, I present to you the Wedge Document, unedited and in its entirety. And for those who wish to skim, I've put some of the more intriguing portions in bold.

Enjoy.

CENTER FOR THE RENEWAL
OF SCIENCE & CULTURE

INTRODUCTION

The proposition that human beings are created in the image of God is one of the bedrock principles on which Western civilization was built. Its influence can be detected in most, if not all, of the West's greatest achievements, including representative democracy, human rights, free enterprise, and progress in the arts and sciences.

Yet a little over a century ago, **this cardinal idea came under wholesale attack by intellectuals drawing on the discoveries of modern science.** Debunking the traditional conceptions of both God and man, thinkers such as Charles Darwin, Karl Marx, and Sigmund Freud portrayed humans not as moral and spiritual beings, but as animals or machines who inhabited a universe ruled by purely impersonal forces and whose behavior and very thoughts were dictated by the unbending forces of biology, chemistry, and environment. This materialistic conception of reality eventually infected virtually every area of our culture, from politics and economics to literature and art.

The cultural consequences of this triumph of materialism were devastating. Materialists denied the existence of objective moral standards, claiming that environment dictates our behavior and beliefs. Such moral relativism was uncritically adopted by much of the social sciences, and it still undergirds much of modern economics, political science, psychology and sociology.

Materialists also undermined personal responsibility by asserting that human thoughts and behaviors are dictated by our biology and environment. The results can be seen in modern approaches to criminal justice, product liability, and welfare. In the materialist scheme of things, everyone is a victim and no one can be held accountable for his or her actions.

Finally, materialism spawned a virulent strain of utopianism. Thinking they could engineer the perfect society through the application of scientific knowledge, materialist reformers advocated coercive government programs that falsely promised to create heaven on earth.

Discovery Institute's Center for the Renewal of Science and Culture seeks nothing less than the overthrow of materialism and its cultural legacies. Bringing together leading scholars from the natural sciences and those from the humanities and social sciences, the Center explores how new developments in biology, physics and cognitive science raise serious doubts about scientific materialism and have re-opened the case for a broadly theistic understanding of nature. The Center awards fellowships for original research, holds conferences, and briefs policymakers about the opportunities for life after materialism.

The Center is directed by Discovery Senior Fellow Dr. Stephen Meyer. An Associate Professor of Philosophy at Whitworth College, Dr. Meyer holds a Ph.D.. in the History and Philosophy of Science from Cambridge University. He formerly worked as a geophysicist for the Atlantic Richfield Company.

THE WEDGE STRATEGY

Phase I.
Scientific Research, Writing & Publicity
Phase II.

Publicity & Opinion-making
Phase III.
Cultural Confrontation & Renewal

THE WEDGE PROJECTS

Phase I.
Scientific Research, Writing & Publication
• Individual Research Fellowship Program • Paleontology Research program (Dr. Paul Chien et al.) • Molecular Biology Research Program (Dr. Douglas Axe et al.)

Phase II.
Publicity & Opinion-making
• Book Publicity
• Opinion-Maker Conferences
• Apologetics Seminars
• Teacher Training Program
• Op-ed Fellow
• PBS (or other TV) Co-production
• Publicity Materials / Publications

Phase III.
Cultural Confrontation & Renewal
• Academic and Scientific Challenge Conferences • **Potential Legal Action for Teacher Training** • Research Fellowship Program: shift to social sciences and humanities

FIVE YEAR STRATEGIC PLAN SUMMARY
The social consequences of materialism have been devastating. As symptoms, those consequences are certainly worth treating. **However, we are convinced that in order to defeat materialism, we must cut it off at its source. That source is scientific materialism. This is precisely our strategy. If we view the predominant materialistic science as a giant tree, our strat-**

egy is intended to function as a "wedge" that, while relatively small, can split the trunk when applied at its weakest points. The very beginning of this strategy, the "thin edge of the wedge," was Phillip Johnson's critique of Darwinism begun in 1991 in Darwinism on Trial, and continued in Reason in the Balance and Defeating Darwinism by Opening Minds. Michael Behe's highly successful Darwin's Black Box followed Johnson's work. We are building on this momentum, broadening the wedge with a positive scientific alternative to materialistic scientific theories, which has come to be called the theory of Intelligent Design (ID). **Design theory promises to reverse the stifling dominance of the materialist worldview, and to replace it with a science consonant with Christian and theistic convictions.**

The Wedge strategy can be divided into three distinct but interdependent phases, which are roughly but not strictly chronological. We believe that, with adequate support, we can accomplish many of the objectives of Phases I and II in the next five years (1999-2003), and begin Phase III (See "Goals/ Five Year Objectives/Activities").

Phase I: Research, Writing and Publication, Phase II: Publicity and Opinion-making, Phase III: Cultural Confrontation and Renewal

Phase I is the essential component of everything that comes afterward. Without solid scholarship, research and argument, the project would be just another attempt to indoctrinate instead of persuade. A lesson we have learned from the history of science is that it is unnecessary to outnumber the opposing establishment. Scientific revolutions are usually staged by an initially small and relatively young group of scientists who are not blinded by the prevailing prejudices and who are able to do creative work at the pressure points, that is, on those critical issues upon which whole systems of thought hinge. So, in Phase I we are supporting vital writing and research at the sites most likely to crack the materialist edifice.

Phase II. The primary purpose of Phase II is to prepare the popular reception of our ideas. **The best and truest research can languish unread and unused unless it is properly publicized. For this reason we seek to cultivate and convince influential individuals in print and broadcast media, as well as think tank leaders, scientists and academics, congressional staff, talk show hosts, college and seminary presidents and faculty, future talent and potential academic allies.** Because of his long tenure in politics, journalism and public policy, Discovery President Bruce Chapman brings to the project rare knowledge and acquaintance of key op-ed writers, journalists, and political leaders. This combination of scientific and scholarly expertise and media and political connections makes the Wedge unique, and also prevents it from being "merely academic." Other activities include production of a PBS documentary on Intelligent Design and its implications, and popular op-ed publishing. **Alongside a focus on influential opinion-makers, we also seek to build up a popular base of support among our natural constituency, namely, Christians. We will do this primarily through apologetics seminars. We intend these to encourage and equip believers with new scientific evidences that support the faith, as well as to "popularize" our ideas in the broader culture.**

Phase III. Once our research and writing have had time to mature, and the public prepared for the reception of design theory, we will move toward direct confrontation with the advocates of materialist science through challenge conferences in significant academic settings. **We will also pursue possible legal assistance in response to resistance to the integration of design theory into public school science curricula.** The attention, publicity, and influence of design theory should draw scientific materialists into open debate with design theorists, and we will be ready. With an added emphasis to the social sciences and humanities, we will begin to address the specific social consequences of materialism and the Darwinist theory that supports it in the sciences.

GOALS

Governing Goals
• To defeat scientific materialism and its destructive moral, cultural and political legacies.
• To replace materialistic explanations with the theistic understanding that nature and human beings are created by God.

Five Year Goals
• To see Intelligent Design theory as an accepted alternative in the sciences and scientific research being done from the perspective of design theory.
• To see the beginning of the influence of design theory in spheres other than natural science.
• To see major new debates in education, life issues, legal and personal responsibility pushed to the front of the national agenda.

Twenty Year Goals
• **To see Intelligent Design theory as the dominant perspective in science. • To see design theory application in specific fields, including molecular biology, biochemistry, paleontology, physics and cosmology in the natural sciences, psychology, ethics, politics, theology and philosophy in the humanities; to see its influence in the fine arts. • To see design theory permeate our religious, cultural, moral and political life.**

FIVE YEAR OBJECTIVES

1. A major public debate between design theorists and Darwinists (by 2003)

2. Thirty published books on design and its cultural implications (sex, gender issues, medicine, law, and religion)

3. One hundred scientific, academic and technical articles by our fellows

4. Significant coverage in national media: • Cover story on major news magazine such as Time or Newsweek • PBS show such as Nova treating design theory fairly • Regular press coverage on developments in design theory • Favorable op-ed pieces and columns on the design movement by 3rd party media

5. Spiritual & cultural renewal: • Mainline renewal movements begin to appropriate insights from design theory, and to repudiate theologies influenced by materialism • Seminaries increasingly recognize & repudiate naturalistic presuppositions • Positive uptake in public opinion polls on issues such as sexuality, abortion and belief in God

6. Ten states begin to rectify ideological imbalance in their science curricula & include design theory

7. Scientific achievements • An active design movement in Israel, the UK and other influential countries outside the US • Ten CRSC Fellows teaching at major universities • Two universities where design theory has become the dominant view • Design becomes a key concept in the social sciences • **Legal reform movements base legislative proposals on design theory**

Okay, I'm back. Quite a piece of work, eh? Personally, I would have punched it up a bit with some wacky metaphors and maybe a bizarre tirade against Constantine and the Byzantine Empire or something, but, you know, "live and let live," as a non-evangelical might say.

You get the picture, though. Nonetheless, there are a few specific points that should be addressed. The Reader will have noticed that among the "Five-Year Objectives" listed above, one of the chief among these is that "Ten states begin to rectify ideological imbalance in their science curricula & include design theory." Which is to say, the Discovery Institute would very much like to see ten states "include design theory" in their public school curricula. And because this is listed as a "Five-Year Objective," one might reasonably assume that this is some sort of "objective" that the Discovery Institute was working to fulfill, preferably within five years.

Now, bearing that in mind, the Reader is now invited to "surf the 'net," as the kids say, and, in doing so, to stop off at **www.discovery.org**, the Discovery Institute's official website. Under the "Frequently Asked Questions" section, the Reader will find the following frequently asked question, as well as the presumably frequently answered answer:

3. Should public schools require the teaching of Intelligent Design?
No. Instead of mandating Intelligent Design, Discovery Institute recommends that states and school districts focus on teaching students more about evolutionary theory, including telling them about some of the theory's problems that have been discussed in peer-reviewed science journals. In other words, evolution should be taught as a scientific theory that is open to critical scrutiny, not as a sacred dogma that can't be questioned. We believe this is a common-sense approach that will benefit students, teachers, and parents.

Gee, that's strange. It's almost as if these two stances contradict each other. One might even assume that the secret "Five-Year Plan" – er, uh, "Objective" – is actually the true aim of the Discovery Institute, while the frequently answered answer is meant to present a slightly more reasonable face to the public.

And then there's this other Wedge Document gem: "We will also pursue possible legal assistance in response to resistance to the integration of design theory into public school science curricula." Resistance is futile.

The Reader may also have noticed another "Five-Year Objective": "Legal reform movements base legislative proposals on design theory." God only knows what that's supposed to mean. Maybe we can get William Dembski to ask Him for us.

Moving right along, we also have this: "Design theory promises to reverse the stifling dominance of the materialist worldview, and to replace it with a science consonant with Christian and theistic convictions." That, of course, is also from the Wedge Document, and not from the Discovery Institute web site, which claims that said institution "is a secular think tank" and "a non-partisan policy and research organization."

But all of these telling discrepancies, while certainly telling and discrepant, are secondary to the underlying fact: real scientific institutions do not base their work around any sort of preconceived social agenda. Real scientific institutions do not "seek to cultivate and convince influential individuals in print and broadcast media, as well as think tank leaders, scientists and academics, congressional staff, talk show hosts, college and seminary presidents and faculty, future talent and potential academic allies," as the authors of this document do. Real scientific institutions do not work to "defeat" prevailing scientific frameworks, nor do they vow to "split the trunk" by driving a "wedge" into its "weakest points." Real scientific institutions do not aim to parlay their alliances with "influential opinion-makers" into a PR machine intended to "build up a popular base of support" among their "natural constituency," because real scientific institutions do not have natural constituencies, and particularly not ones that happen to fall under religion lines – in the case of the Discovery Institute, "namely, Christians." Real scientific institutions do not hold "apologetics seminars." Real scientific institutions do not "encourage and equip" their "believers" with haphazard pseudoscience in order to "support the faith."

Rather, these are the sorts of things that religious zealots do.

***

The Discovery Institute has certainly done a fine job of getting Intelligent Design onto the public radar. They've even managed to score a cover story in *Time*, just like O.J. Simpson once did. In fact, the scientific case for Intelligent Design is actually rather compelling when it's adulterated with fabrications, purged of inconvenient facts, and presented directly to the scientifically illiterate American public.

Or, as the Discovery Institute might put it if they were to quote me:

> "The Discovery Institute has certainly done a fine job of getting Intelligent Design onto the public radar," Brown wrote. "They've even managed to score a cover story in *Time*...In fact, the scientific case for Intelligent Design is actually rather compelling when it's...presented directly to the...American public."

Think I'm exaggerating? Frankly, I'm hurt. But don't take it from me. Just ask the National Center for Science Education.

A few years back, the Discovery Institute decided that the state of Ohio could use a little help with their public school science curriculum, which they felt was far too weighted towards established scientific theories, like the theory of evolution and, presumably, the theory of gravity, both of which, after all, are "just theories." To this end, they decided to compile a helpful list of peer-reviewed papers by scientists more respectable than the ones associated with the Discovery Institute. This, they believed, would assuredly shed the light of the Logos on all of Ohio. The resulting document, entitled "Bibliography of Supplementary Resources for Ohio Science Education," was submitted to the appropriate Ohioan administrators, along with the following preface:

> "The publications represent dissenting viewpoints that challenge one or another aspect of neo-Darwinism (the prevailing theory of evolution taught in biology textbooks), discuss problems that evolutionary theory faces, or suggest important new lines of evidence that biology must consider when explaining origins."

When the folks at the National Center for Science Education caught wind of this, they were naturally suspicious. And so the NCSE sent a questionnaire to each of the scientists whose work had been included in the bibliography, asking said scientists if they believed that their work provided support for Intelligent Design. Of the 26 scientists who responded, not a single one said that this was the case. In fact, as the NCSE put it, "many were indignant at the suggestion." Here's a sampling:

> **David P. Mindell:** "The words enclosed in quotation marks are accurate. However, the quotes are entirely misinterpreted and taken out of context. This is just as the scientific community, and at least some of the public, has come to expect from the Discovery Institute."

> **Kenneth Weiss:** "I state clearly that evolution

is beyond dispute based on all the evidence I am aware of."

Douglas H. Erwin: "Of course not – [Intelligent Design] is a non sequitur, nothing but a fundamentally flawed attempt to promote creationism under a different guise. Nothing in this paper or any of my other work provides the slightest scintilla of support for *Intelligent Design*. To argue that it does requires a deliberate and pernicious misreading of the papers."

Douglas L. Erwin (no relation): "While the article considers the relationship between micro- and macro- evolution, the statement above is inaccurate in saying that I am challenging the standard view of evolution. The treatment of macro-evolution in that paper is an extension [of evolutionary theory], but by no means a challenge."

David M. Williams: "The short answer to your question, 'Do you consider this accurate?' is no."

And there you have it.

After the NCSE made this public, the Discovery Institute added the following disclaimer to the website version of its haphazard bibliography:

"The publications are not presented either as support for the theory of Intelligent Design, or as indicating that the authors cited doubt evolution. Discovery Institute has made every effort to ensure that the annotated summaries accurately reflect the central arguments of the publications."

That would certainly seem to contradict the original preface, which stated just the opposite. And that second sentence is just plainly wrong. But, hey, we all make mistakes. Sometimes we make a couple dozen huge, intentional mistakes, compile them into a bibliography, and send it all off to Ohio. Sometimes we don't. It's all a part of growing up, like smashing freestanding mailboxes with a baseball bat from the passenger seat of a 1976 Mustang. But, ideally, we also learn from these mistakes. The Discovery Institute does not. And that's why even after that whole bibliography debacle, Discovery Institute bigwig Stephen Meyer still occasionally makes the claim that the documents pointed to in the bibliography "raise significant challenges to key tenets of Darwinian evolution."

So how many scientists really question the basic tenets of evolution without having to find out about it from an NCSE questionnaire? Since 2001, the Discovery Institute has maintained a list of "doctoral scientists, researchers and theorists at a number of universities, colleges, and research institutes around the world" who have been willing to sign on to its "Scientific Dissent from Darwin" statement, which reads, "We are skeptical of claims for the ability of random mutation and natural selection to account for the complexity of life. Careful examination of the evidence for Darwinian theory should be encouraged." So far, they've managed to rack up "over 300 scientists," which is, uh, great, and which would be even more impressive if by "scientist," they didn't include just anyone with "a Ph.D. in engineering, mathematics, computer science, biology, chemistry, or one of the other natural sciences," which, incidentally, they do.

Hearing of this, those incorrigible scamps over at the National Center for Science Education decided it was time to strike again. In 2003, the NCSE unveiled "Project Steve," by which anyone with the name "Steve," Steven," "Stephen," "Stephan," or "Stephanie" who possesses a Ph.D. "in biology, geology, paleontology, or a related scientific field," which is to say, a field touching directly upon evolution, and not computer science or something was invited to sign on to the following statement:

> "Evolution is a vital, well-supported, unifying principle of the biological sciences, and the scientific evidence is overwhelmingly in favor of the idea that all living things share a common ancestry. Although there are legitimate debates about the patterns and processes of evolution, there is no serious scientific doubt that evolution occurred or that natural selection is a major mechanism in its occurrence. It is scientifically inappropriate and pedagogically irresponsible for creationist pseudoscience, including but not limited to 'Intelligent Design,' to be introduced into the science curricula of our nation's public schools."

To date almost 1000 Steves had signed the statement.

* * *

In a fundamental sense, it really doesn't matter if advocates of Intelligent Design are outnumbered by a factor of a million, a thousand, or ten. Science is not a democracy, which is why, unlike a democracy, science works. Science produces results. Science produces those results by maintaining the integrity of the scientific method. And one of the key elements to scientific inquiry is the process of peer review; whereby a scientific work is examined for inaccuracies, by other scientists with appropriate credentials, before being published.

Those with a particular fondness for court transcripts were treated to an interesting discussion on peer review during that wacky Dover trial we discussed in the first chapter. So that the court might get a better sense of the issues involved, none other than Michael Behe, author of the aforementioned *Darwin's Black Box*, was asked to testify regarding the alleged scientific merits of Intelligent Design. And, just like William Buckingham before him, Behe ended up being humiliated by ACLU attorney Eric Rothschild, who spent much of his cross-examination pointing out the various flaws and limitations inherent in Behe's attempts to prove the existence of irreducible complexity.

Among other things, Behe was forced to admit that much of the material in Black Box failed to account for several important evolutionary mechanisms, that Behe himself had been forced to tweak his original definition of irreducible complexity, that Behe had on at least one occasion mixed up the terms "biological" and "biochemical" in passages where the differences in meaning would have been crucial, that "Intelligent Design does not rule out natural explanations," and, perhaps best of all, that "There are no peer reviewed articles by anyone advocating for Intelligent Design supported by pertinent experiments or calculations which provide detailed rigorous accounts of how Intelligent Design of any biological system occurred."

If *Black Box* and the assumptions entailed therein were so flush with inaccuracies and wholesale silliness, how had the book managed to survive the peer review process? After all, it had allegedly been subject to an unusually rigorous review before publication. As Behe told the court:

> "The review process that the book went through is analogous to peer review in the [scientific] literature, because the manuscript was sent out to scientists for their careful reading. Furthermore, the book was sent out to more sci-

entists than typically review a manuscript. In the typical case, a manuscript that's going to – that is submitted for a publication in a scientific journal is reviewed just by two reviewers. My book was sent out to five reviewers. Furthermore, they read it more carefully than most scientists read typical manuscripts that they get to review because they realized that this was a controversial topic. So I think, in fact, my book received much more scrutiny and much more review before publication than the great majority of scientific journal articles."

Rigorous indeed. Five reviewers is certainly more than two reviewers – three more, according to my preliminary calculations. The only problem is that five reviewers did not read *Black Box*. Only four did. As Rothschild pointed out, alleged reviewer and biochemist Michael Atchison never even saw a copy of the book. Instead, he had been given a short summary of its overriding theme during a ten-minute phone conversation with the publisher, and later explained as much in a newspaper editorial. Still, that leaves four other reviewers – still two more than two. And all four of those remaining reviewers did indeed read the book, which is certainly an important step when it comes to reviewing things.

A few pro-Darwinist individuals associated with the website "Panda's Thumb" were curious as to what the others had thought about the book. So they e-mailed reviewers Robert Shapiro, K. John Morrow, and Russell Doolittle, and got interesting replies from each of them.

Robert Shapiro had indeed read the book, but felt that the conclusions were false. As he later wrote:

> "I felt that Professor Behe's book has done a better job of explaining existing science than

others of its kind. I agree with him that conventional scientific origin-of-life theory is deeply flawed. I disagreed with him about the idea that one needed to invoke an Intelligent Designer or a supernatural cause to find an answer. I do not support Intelligent Design theories. I believe that better science will provide the needed answers."

Lukewarm praise, but not entirely dismissive. And then there's K. John Morrow:

"I did review Behe's book for a publisher who turned it down on the basis of my comments, and those of others (including Russell Doolittle who trashed it). When I reviewed Behe's book I was much more polite than Doolittle, who didn't mince words. Eventually Behe found another publisher, so he's right; it was peer reviewed. What he doesn't say is that is was rejected by the first set of reviewers.

I also debated Behe in Dallas in 1992. Once, again, I attempted to be civil, professional and dignified. Behe's response was aggressive, condescending and simply rude.

I will say, unequivocally, I am (as practically every professional working biologist I have every met) convinced by the overwhelming body of evidence that Darwin's concept of evolution, and its subsequent modifications by the last 150 years of investigation, is the correct, and the best explanation for the great cornucopia of living creatures with which we share this planet.

I'm absolutely appalled by Behe's arguments, which are simply a rehash of ideas that Darwin considered and rejected. There is not a shred of evidence to support Intelligent Design, and a vast body of evidence that argues against it. It is not a scientific hypothesis, it is simply the philosophical wanderings of an uniformed (or disingenuous) mind.

At present I'm involved in product development for an immunodiagnostics company, and we are discussing how to approach Avian flu, and how we can design a test that takes into account the constantly evolving nature of the RNA viruses. Do the Intelligent Designers want to return us to a time when mankind attributed disease to evil spirits, and allow us no tools to understand the ravages of epidemic diseases, and how to design therapies and diagnostics against them?

I believe that the argument is not about science at all, but simply right wing fundamentalists using a different tactic to force religious teaching in the public schools. I thought that Judge Overton had put this case to rest 30 years ago, but apparently not."

Yipes. As Morrow notes, Russell Doolittle had very little positive to say about Behe or his book, and seemed particularly peeved that Behe had included Doolittle's own research on blood clotting while apparently misinterpreting the results for his own ends. In 1995, after having read over the manuscript at the request of Morrow, Doolittle wrote back. Wonkish though his letter is, it's worth reprinting here:

"I read the draft of the chapter for a proposed book by Michael Behe that you sent me. As you warned me on the telephone, my own writings play a prominent role in his attack on evolution. I don't know whether the word ingenious or disingenuous is more appropriate here, but he has certainly turned all my thinking completely around to suit his own ends. That it is really disingenuous is clear from the fact that he has managed to belittle important scientific findings by couching them with sarcasm.

But what annoyed me the most in the chapter was the author's appeal to Rube Goldberg, one of my favorite cartoonists, and a person I often refer to for my own perspective. On numerous occasions I have shown the two enclosed Goldberg cartoons as examples of how evolution works! Indeed, I used them in (trying to) teach our medical students about how complicated cascades work in contemporary cells. Also, I have used the same cartoons in debating our local creationist (Duane Gish), pointing out that certainly no Creator would have designed such a circuitous and contrived system. Instead, this is how the opportunistic hand of natural selection works, using whatever happens to be available at the moment. (I wonder if he knew about this?)

But let me back up a bit. First, the 1993 article of mine, which is so heavily quoted from and intentionally disparaged, was the text of a lecture I presented at an international conference on blood clotting. It was presented to an audience of mainly clinicians and biotechnologists, not persons well versed in the rudiments of protein evolution. The tone was intentionally light and breezy. My 'casual language' has to be viewed in this light. My main point was to demonstrate that the delicate balance of forward and backward reactions that regulate blood clotting came about in a step-by-step process. I emphasized that the Yin-Yang was simply a metaphor and that other similar point and counterpoint comparisons could be made.

A more rigorous development of these ideas can be found in the cited references, one of which (Doolittle & Feng, 1987) is enclosed. This article predicted that certain components of the cascade appear relatively late in vertebrate evolution, and data in support of this contention are just now forthcoming (lower vertebrates appear to lack the equivalents of factors XI and XII).

A wonderful example of how gene duplications operate in this regard was noted almost 25 years ago. Thus, in hemoglobin, similar sequence extrapolations backwards in time suggested that the gene duplication leading to alpha and beta chains occurred at about the time of the diversification of fishes (see Fig. 1 of Doolittle, 1987, (enclosed). Indeed, when hemoglobin from lampreys and hagfish were examined, they were found to be single-\|chained! They had diverged before the key alpha /beta duplication that has led to the allosteric regulation of oxygen transport. Max Perutz has written elegantly about this.

Here are a few of his comments that I found most irritating.

On page IV-29 the author bold-facedly claims that 'the (Doolittle) article does not explain.. how clotting might have originated and subsequently evolved.' and then in italics '..no one on earth has the vaguest idea how the co-agulation cascade came to be.'

I disagree. I have a good idea, shared by most workers in the field, and it is a matter of the (important) details that we are trying to establish.

On page IV-24, Behe underscores that no "causative factors are cited.' 'What exactly is causing all this springing and unleashing?' Gene duplications, of course, the frequency of which is difficult to measure (I often note that 'duplication begets more duplication,' for reasons of the misalignment of similar sequences), but which is turning out to be enormously more common than expected.

Causation is tricky. Sometimes environmental or internal benefits are obvious. Often however, the rule for survival is 'no harm, no foul,' with adaptations occurring subsequently. For the moment, they don't even have to be slightly improved.

As for the 'enormous luck needed,' we are now into the crux of all evolutionary problems, which is to say, what is the probability of survival? Population geneticists are attempting to answer such questions in general terms (see, e.g., J. B. Walsh, Genetics, 139, 421-428, 1995). In fact, the product of most gene duplications, which are the heart of the evolutionary process, are doomed to random oblivion (see enclosed, Doolittle, Science, 1981).

Also, on page IV-26, he states, 'the crucial issues of how much? how fast? when? where?' are not addressed. These are relevant and not unknowable matters. There is a wonderful article about to appear in Molecular Phylogenetics by D. Gumucio et al on how fetal hemoglobin has evolved in primates and that also outlines exactly the regulatory circumstances that allow its differential expression. Finally, my 'model' does give some important numbers. The power of sequence-based analysis is that it reveals the order of appearance of new proteins, even when the sequences are limited to one or a few species. As noted above, it also has the power to make predictions about the occurrence of proteins in different creatures.

In the meantime, we must ask Mr. Behe whether he doubts the existence of gene duplications? (There are many examples of closely related species where one has n copies of a gene and the other m.) If he acknowledges their existence, then how does he account for the pseudogenes that these duplications often give rise to? Does he think they have a function? And what does he think was the origin of allosteric hemoglobins in all but the most primitive vertebrates? As I say, even his derisive comments call attention to a system that could only have come about by natural selection.

Should the book be published? Scurrilous as it is, I am a believer in a free press. I also know most publishers will publish anything that can make money, and I'm sure there's a naive market for claptrap like this.

I only ask that if you do recommend publication that you suggest that I be invited to review the book, so I can put my own Rube Goldberg cartoons to use."

That's one mad scientist. At any rate, Doolittle's prediction turned out to be accurate. *Darwin's Black Box* did indeed see publication - by a different publisher with 'different' standards.

* * *

Gentle Reader, I do hope you will forgive me for the gargantuan single paragraph that I am about to impart on you, but I felt the meaning was best delivered in one breathless outburst:

The intent of the Discovery Institute is simple enough. It desires to restore the United States to an idyllic state of being that never existed, and it seeks to accomplish this by reviving a theocratic philosophy that its founders never held. It seeks to remind its modern citizenry that this nation was founded on a particular religion even though this nation was the first in human history to be founded on no particular religion at all. It seeks to further this goal by attacking a theory that is more than a theory and replacing it with another that is less than one. And to accomplish that, it is willing to claim that its empty concepts have received above-average peer review when nothing could be further from the truth; it is willing to cast the secondary debates over certain evolutionary mechanisms as the death knell of a "theory in crisis," while at the same time seeking to downplay the fact that intelligent design's backers can't seem to agree on whether the Earth is thousands of years old or millions; it is willing to mischaracterize the results achieved by real scientists in order to achieve short-lived propaganda victories, and it is willing to continue to do so even after these real scientists object and even after it has apologized and promised to stop doing so. Above all, it is willing to cloak its true socio-political goals behind a consciously-crafted veil of dispassionate scientific inquiry, even while denouncing science itself. If the Discovery

Institute tells a lie, it does so in order to advance the Truth. Because the Discovery Institute fights for morality, it is above morality.

Indeed, the intent of the Discovery Institute is simple enough. Con men are rarely complicated.

SIX

So You've Decided to Take a Stand for Science!

The way to deal with superstition is not to be polite to it, but to tackle it with all arms, and so rout it, cripple it, and make it forever infamous and ridiculous. Is it, perchance, cherished by persons who should know better? Then their folly should be brought out into the light of day, and exhibited there in all its hideousness until they flee from it, hiding their heads in shame.

– H.L. Mencken

Okay, so everyone's nuts except for you and I. And when I go to bed at night, I always make sure that my legs are entirely under the covers so that the monsters can't get me; and thus, I too am nuts. That just leaves you, the Reader. So what exactly are you, the Reader, planning to do about all of this Intelligent Design nonsense?

One thing you can do is sit around and enjoy the show. While it's certainly true that a majority of Americans are supporters of either creationism or creationism's post-adolescent older sibling, Intelligent Design, this need not necessarily translate into any horrible national policy implementations. According to a recent *Newsweek* poll, for example, more than half of Americans believe in the Rapture, but Congress has yet to make any appropriations for a viable post-apocalypse governmental framework. Obviously, some of this planning is just common sense and requires little forethought; the remaining members of the Republican and Democratic parties, for example, would of course be led by Arlen Specter and Joseph Lieberman, respectively. But there still doesn't seem to be any viable strategy in place for the inevitable confrontation with Gog and Magog, to say nothing of all those locusts. And our military appears to be bogged down in Babylon for reasons that temporarily escape me. In essence, our devoutly religious fellow-citizens are quite serious about their beliefs regarding the future, though not so serious that they're necessarily going to act on any of them.

Or perhaps this preponderance of non-planning simply means that our pious countrymen don't really give a damn about those of us who will be left to the locusts. In fact, that's probably it. And thus maybe we should concern ourselves with the possibility that the Intelligent Design proponents are inclined to the point of real action to get their pseudo-scientific silliness pushed into the national scientific consciousness in a way that actually, you know, matters.

If that's the case, and if you're truly keen on fulfilling your patriotic duty to protect the Nation of the Enlightenment from the Legions of Tomfoolery, then you'd better bone up on the movers and shakers of the anti-evolution movement. To this end, I've prepared the following guide to some of the nation's most misguided medievalists.

Philip E. Johnson

The father of the Intelligent Design movement, a co-founder of the Discovery Institute, and, of course, a Biblical literalist, Johnson is also an accomplished law professor who once taught at UC Berkley, where he was presumably driven insane by that locale's notorious penchant for hyper-secularism. The modern use of the term "Intelligent Design" may be traced to Johnson's 1991 book, "Darwin on Trial," in which Darwin was found guilty by no less an impartial jury than Johnson himself. In addition, Johnson is also the author, literally and otherwise, of the Wedge Strategy. And in the damning quotes department, he's second only to William Dembski. My personal favorite is his famous remark that "[t]his isn't really, and never has been, a debate about science. It's about religion and philosophy."

The Reader need not worry about Johnson doing any further damage, though, as he is currently in the process of dying, and may very well be dead by the time you read this book. This is because he's suffered from several strokes over the last few years. Please don't think me callous for trampling on the decrepit; my only intent is to educate the Reader, and Johnson's misfortunes are very educational indeed. The following is from Kevin Condon, an apparent friend of the family and obvious Bible junkie:

> "The stroke made him realize that much of his 'fun' in Intelligent Design argument and ID leadership had not been about anything more than his personal pride, the pleasure of the battle and the devastating rhetorical moves he was able to make in besting his opponents. With the help of his church and his wife Kathie, Johnson realized that the stroke he suffered was a gift from God. Jesus was calling him to a closer walk by shaking the false foundation he had built upon his own intellect and cleverness. His stroke put the permanence of his dependably superior intellectual gifts in jeopardy."

One has to wonder if that was the diagnosis. "Mrs. Johnson, I'm afraid that your husband has come down with a gift from God." Are you supposed to treat something like that, or just let God's will take its mysterious course? At any rate, it's probably nothing a few leeches can't fix.

Something like this actually happened to me a while back. I came down with a sinus infection, and I realized that God was trying to get me to spend more time indoors so that I would have more time in which to do His work, which itself involves taking cheap shots at elderly stroke victims. Of course, my mother kept calling and telling me to take antibiotics, but I knew that this was another sign from God that I shouldn't take any antibiotics at all, because it was, like, Opposite Day or something.

Stephen C. Meyer

Meyer is kind of a third-wheel in a greater Holy Trinity of Intelligent Design consisting of himself, William Dembski, and Michael Behe. In the war for America's soul, Meyer generally gets stuck writing disingenuous op-ed columns. He also happens to resemble a dinosaur, but not in a good way.

Meyer's background is in geology; before making the jump to full-time culture war conductor, he first worked in the petroleum business. He also once won a scholarship to Cambridge, which is pretty impressive. On the other hand, it should also be remembered that Francis Ford Coppola directed *The Godfather II* before he directed *The Godfather III*, if you catch my drift.

Meyer scored a major public relations coup when he managed to get a pro-Intelligent Design paper published in the peer-reviewed Proceeding of the Biological Society of Washington. Unfortunately, the paper was quickly disowned. Here's an explanatory press release from the PBSW itself:

> *The paper by Stephen C. Meyer, "The origin of biological information and the higher taxonomic categories," in vol. 117, no. 2, pp. 213-239*

of the Proceedings of the Biological Society of Washington, was published at the discretion of the former editor, Richard V. Sternberg. Contrary to typical editorial practices, the paper was published without review by any associate editor; Sternberg handled the entire review process. The Council, which includes officers, elected councilors, and past presidents, and the associate editors would have deemed the paper inappropriate for the pages of the Proceedings because the subject matter represents such a significant departure from the nearly purely systematic content for which this journal has been known throughout its 122-year history. For the same reason, the journal will not publish a rebuttal to the thesis of the paper, the superiority of Intelligent Design (ID) over evolution as an explanation of the emergence of Cambrian body-plan diversity.

The editor who had published the paper contrary to standard review procedure, Richard Sternberg, also happens to be a fellow at the International Society for Complexity, Information and Design, a pro-Intelligent Design organization that was co-founded by none other than William Dembski.

Small world, isn't it?

William Dembski

William Dembski is probably the most perpetually active Intelligent Design proponent to date. He's written quite a few books, most of which appear to have been published by InterVarsity, that goofy evangelical activism outfit that's done such fine work raising public awareness of evil spirits and Mediterranean demons. But give the devil his due; one of Dembski's earlier works, *The Design Inference*, was published by Cambridge University Press, which is decidedly more, ahem, respectable than InterVarsity. In fact, the book was even peer-reviewed – by philosophers.

There are two important things that the Reader must remember about William Dembski. The first thing to remember about William Dembski is that William Dembski considers the eye to be so wonderfully constructed that its existence can only be accounted for by an omnipotent Intelligent Designer with infinite resources and unlimited foresight. The second thing to remember about William Dembski is that William Dembski wears glasses.

But William Dembski is more than a walking contradiction. He's also grossly inept. In one of his books, *No Free Lunch: Why Specified Complexity Cannot Be Purchased without Intelligence*, Dembski bases his arguments on the No Free Lunch Theorem, which itself was originally developed by physicists David Wolpert and William Macready. But after reading Dembski's take on the subject, Wolpert characterized the fellow's reasoning as having been "written in jello," and further described the book's arguments as "fatally informal and imprecise." In summary, "There simply is not enough that is firm in his text, not sufficient precision of formulation, to allow one to declare unambiguously 'right' or 'wrong' when reading through the argument. All one can do is squint, furrow one's brows, and then shrug." Which is not to say that the book's reception was entirely negative; many evangelical Christians seemed to have really enjoyed it.

In essence, Dembski has the consistency of Timothy Leary, and occasionally sounds like him, too. In *Intelligent Design*, for instance, Dembski is kind enough to tell us the following: "I look at a blade of grass and it speaks to me. In the light of the sun, it tells me that it is green." Dude, that is so true! Also, did you know you can make a hash pipe out of an apple?

Nor is Dembski's attempted muscling-in limited only to

science and the drug culture – history class is next. As Dembski once wrote, "Predictive prophecies in Scripture are instances of specified complexity and signal information inputted by God as part of his sovereign activity within Creation." So, you know, get ready for all those murderous pseudo-locusts. I suggest wearing long sleeves. And I'm sure the world's astronomers will be interested to see all those stars fall to Earth, as predicted in the *Book of Revelation*s. I wonder if Dembski is aware that a single star is many orders of magnitude larger than our planet, and that the first star to "fall" would destroy all life on Earth before it even managed to "land." Gee, if I didn't know better, I'd say the *Book of Revelation*s was written by someone who had no fucking idea what he was talking about. "Instances of specified complexity and signal information inputted by God." Christ, what a piece of work.

Speaking of Christ, I was personally very irritated to discover that Dembski advocates something that he calls "Christology," because I had actually hoped to coin the term myself and then use it as a pejorative against Dembski himself. I guess I was too late, though. Which is to say, if Christology didn't exist, man would have had to invent it.

Don't ask me to describe what Christology is, though, because I wouldn't know how to go about it. This is what theologians like William Dembski are for. As far as I can tell from Dembski's glowing description in *Intelligent Design*, it involves the "word-flesh," "Hermeneutic principles," and the subordination of our entire scientific infrastructure to a theocratic junta led, presumably, by William Dembski. But don't worry, kids. "This privileging of Christology as the lens through which to view the various disciplines won't violate the integrity of those disciplines." Well, that's a relief. Because I sort of thought that maybe it would.

Ken Ham

Ken Ham sort of looks like a werewolf. He's also one

of the most prominent young-earth creationist scientists in the world. Maybe he ate all the others during the last full moon. I'm sorry, but he really does resemble a werewolf. And for all I know, he believes in werewolves. Why not? He believes in witches. Being a creationist must be very frightening. Especially if you're hanging out with Ken Ham, and he's eating your leg. I'm sorry.

At any rate, Ham is having an impact. What an odd sentence to have to write. Nonetheless, it is true. Ham, after all, is the co-founder of Answers in *Genesis*, an organization dedicated to telling you that you will find various answers in the *Book of Genesis*, which is actually true if the question is, "Where can I find interesting stories about giants raping Earth women?" More importantly, AIG is also dedicated to subverting the nation's science classes through sabotage, to be carried out by children. It's an interesting strategy, and not entirely an unusual one, although it's generally more likely to be practiced among Central African warlords rather than alleged scientists.

L.A. Times staff writer Stephanie Simon wrote a wonderful piece on Ham's popular creationist seminars, which he holds for both children and adults. The latter he riles up by saying things like, "I'm going to arm you with Christian Patriot missiles!" That particular line is assuredly a great hit with the fellows. Of course, when he's talking to the kiddos, he has to dumb it down a little:

> *In a bit that brought the house down, Ham flashed a picture of a chimpanzee. "Did your grandfather look like this?" he demanded.*
> *"Noooooo!" the children called.*
> *"And did your grandmother look like that?" Ham displayed a photo of the same chimp wearing lipstick. The children erupted in giggles. "Nooooooo!"*

Really in his element, isn't he? We could screw up half his act by passing some sort of law making it a crime to apply lipstick to a chimpanzee. That really should be illegal, anyway. I don't think it's covered by the First Amendment. If you happen to go to mass with Justice Scalia or share the same wholesale gorgonzola distributor or something like that, be sure and ask him for me.

Imagine a methodological naturalist trying to do a seminar like this:

> Methodological Naturalist: *Hey, kids! Did you know that the fossil record, coupled with advances in radiometric dating techniques, observable processes of speciation among insects, and literally hundreds of thousands of pieces of physical evidence accumulated within dozens of accepted scientific disciplines, clearly indicates that all life on Earth derives from a common ancestor?*
>
> Kids: ...
>
> Methodological Naturalist: *Also, there's no such thing as Santa Claus! The concept of Santa Claus actually derives from a popular Northern European tradition dating back several hundred years, although the figure of Santa Claus himself is indeed based on the historical Saint Nicholas...*
> (Teacher politely asks Methodological Naturalist to leave.)

The overriding purpose of Ken Ham's child-targeted seminars is to instruct kids on how to disrupt science classes with literalist Christian propaganda – and shoddy literalist

Christian propaganda at that.

From Simon's piece:

> *"Boys and girls," Ham said. If a teacher so much as mentions evolution, or the Big Bang, or an era when dinosaurs ruled the Earth, "you put your hand up and you say, 'Excuse me, were you there?' Can you remember that?"*
>
> *The children roared their assent.*
>
> *"Sometimes people will answer, 'No, but you weren't there either,'" Ham told them. "Then you say, 'No, I wasn't, but I know someone who was, and I have his book about the history of the world.'" He waved his Bible in the air.*
> *"Who's the only one who's always been there?" Ham asked.*
> *"God!" the boys and girls shouted.*
> *"Who's the only one who knows everything?"*
> *"God!"*
> *"So who should you always trust, God or the scientists?"*
> *The children answered with a thundering: "God!"*

Unfortunately, God is unlikely to show up in your child's science class in order to testify to the truth of all this, so we'll just have to settle for Ken Ham.

So, how are the nation's creationist kiddos carrying out their bombing runs? The answer may be found in yet another Stephanie Simon piece (apparently, she's got the *L.A. Times* "wacko" beat, which must be quite demanding when the paper you're employed with is based in California). The setting is a

Missouri high school biology class, taught by a teacher named
Al Frisby:

> *As his students rummage for their notebooks,
> Frisby introduces his central theme: Every
> creature on Earth has been shaped by random
> mutation and natural selection — in a word, by
> evolution. The challenges begin at once.*
>
> *"Isn't it true that mutations only make an
> animal weaker?" sophomore Chris Willett
> demands. "'Cause I was watching one time
> on CNN and they mutated monkeys to see if
> they could get one to become human and they
> couldn't."*

He was probably thinking of Fox. But it gets worse:

> *Frisby tries to explain that evolution takes
> millions of years, but Willett isn't listening. "I
> feel a tail growing!" he calls to his friends,
> drawing laughter.*

First of all, let us all hope, for the good of the Republic,
that most high school biology teachers do not go by the name of
"Mr. Frisby," because, if so, our battle is already lost. Secondly,
let's hope that, as soon as the reporter left, Mr. Frisby (shortened
from "Flying Novelty Disk" upon the family's arrival at Ellis Is-
land) gave this Chris Willett fellow a thorough paddling for dis-
rupting the class with horrible one-liners. I'm talking a "Board
of Education" beat-down straight out of a Roald Dahl novel.
The ol' Dickens metronome. Oh, he'll "feel a tail growing," all
right. And thirdly, is this what passes for class clownism among
creationists?

Of course, corporal punishment is now the exception,
not the rule, and besides, I'm sure Mr. Frisby is a very nice fel-

low and would never resort to such measures in this sort of circumstance. Nonetheless, we may hope that this particular high school is equipped with a gang of methodological naturalist bullies who will beat up this Chris Willett kid at recess, and then perhaps take his lunch money and use it to buy microscopes or subscriptions to *Scientific American* or something.

"I think I feel a tail growing!" Yeah, kid. And I think I'm coming down with a bad case of stigmata.

Don't blame Chris Willet, though. Blame Ken Ham. In fact, just avoid Ken Ham in general, because he is a werewolf, and he will eat you. Worse, if he just bites you, then you yourself will also turn into a werewolf. I think that's in the Bible. Or, if not, it should be.

Answers in *Genesis*

As mentioned above, Ken Ham's Answers in *Genesis* organization is leading the battle for our nation's high school science courses, among other things. I would recommend that the Reader visit **www.answersinGenesis.com** and check out what passes for intelligent social discourse in that particular organization. Here, I'll get you started with one of my favorites: an article by Carl Kerby, "a former air traffic controller at Chicago's busy O'Hare International Airport" who is now employed as a "dynamic creation speaker." Are you ready? You probably think you're ready, but you're not. Nothing can prepare you for this sort of thing. At any rate, you're as ready as you'll ever be. Here's the excerpt:

> "I'll discuss a few examples of how Hollywood has slipped in evolutionary content to make us think of it as fact. Did you know that evolution can be found in classic TV Land shows like *The Munsters*? In the episode 'Herman the Master Spy,' a Russian fishing trawler picks up a scuba-diving Herman in its haul of fish and

mistakes him for the missing link."

Kerby, it's *The Munsters*. The kid is a werewolf. Herman is a Frankenstein sort of thing. Grandpa is a perverted vampire. The wife is one of those high-maintenance brunettes I always end up getting involved with for some reason. They're all evil, ungodly creatures, presented in a positive light. That's what you should be focusing on as a Christian. Besides, those godless Russian fishermen mistake him for the missing link, and so perhaps 'Herman the Master Spy' was actually a thinly-veiled creationist satire on those past taxidermy-related mishaps that evolutionists have occasionally made. More likely, it was simply written by some no-talent smack addict, just like every other sitcom in human history. But the important thing to grasp here is that Carl Kerby is sitting on a couch somewhere, watching Nick at Nite with notepad in hand, attempting to unravel a conspiracy that doesn't exist.

Also, I suppose it would be kind of nit-picky of me to point out that a "trawler," being an inanimate object, is not actually a sentient entity, and is therefore incapable of "mistaking" Herman Munster for anything. And so I won't do that. But can you believe that I just wrote that sentence? If you had told me a few years ago that I would ever have occasion to point out that a boat is not capable of mistaking Herman Munster for an intermediate species in the hominid evolutionary chain, I would have punched you right in the face for being such a god-damned liar. And then you would have said, "No, seriously, because you're going to be writing about creationists." And then I'd be like, "Oh, right, I guess I can see that." And I would have felt really bad about hitting you, so maybe I'd let you hit me back, just to make things even. But you wouldn't be able to bring yourself to do it. I know you better than that, Gentle Reader.

Ex-Sen. Rick Santorum (R-Pennsylvania)
No American politician has done more for the Intelli-

gent Design movement than Rick Santorum. Actually, that's not true. Thomas Jefferson, by constantly badgering everyone about getting a Bill of Rights thrown in to the Constitution, can actually be considered the father of Intelligent Design. After all, contained in the Bill of Rights is the First Amendment. Contained in the First Amendment is the Establishment Clause. Contained in the Establishment Clause is the idea that the government must not favor one religion over another, even if members of one religion will totally vote for you if you do. And Intelligent Design is an attempt to get around the Establishment Cause, and thus owes its very existence to the Establishment Clause. On the other hand, I like Thomas Jefferson, so I'm not going to lay this at his feet. Instead, I'm going to blame James Madison, who actually ended up drafting the Bill of Rights even though he didn't really want to. Screw you, James Madison. I'm just kidding. I love James Madison.

Anyway, Rick Santorum is second only to that cad James Madison in getting Intelligent Design pushed into the limelight. The proposed Santorum Amendment to the No Child Left Behind Act, for instance, originally consisted of the following:

> *"It is the sense of the Senate that (1) good science education should prepare students to distinguish the data or testable theories of science from philosophical or religious claims that are made in the name of science; and (2) where biological evolution is taught, the curriculum should help students to understand why this subject generates so much continuing controversy, and should prepare the students to be informed participants in public discussions regarding the subject."*

You're probably wondering why this is so poorly worded. The answer is that it was drafted by Philip E. Johnson. Seriously. Later, a second, slightly cleaner version was written by someone who didn't suffer from the handicap of being Philip E. Johnson:

> *"The Conferees recognize that a quality science education should prepare students to distinguish the data and testable theories of science from religious or philosophical claims that are made in the name of science. Where topics are taught that may generate controversy (such as biological evolution), the curriculum should help students to understand the full range of scientific views that exist, why such topics may generate controversy, and how scientific discoveries can profoundly affect society."*

In fact, though, the wording really isn't all that crucial, since the Santorum Amendment didn't end up becoming actual law. Instead, it ended up in what's known as a conference report, and which carries all the legal weight of the instructions on the back of a shampoo bottle. Apparently, no one told this to Rick Santorum, who wrote a 2002 op-ed piece for the *Washington Times* in which he claims the following:

> "At the beginning of the year, President Bush signed into law the 'No Child Left Behind' bill. The new law includes a science education provision where Congress states that 'where topics are taught that may generate controversy (such as biological evolution), the curriculum should help students to understand the full range of scientific views that exist.' If the Education Board of Ohio does not include Intelligent Design in the new teaching standards, many students will

be denied a first-rate science education."

Notice that Rick Santorum is either (a) a liar or (b) ignorant. The Santorum Amendment is not a "provision" of anything. Luckily, this didn't hurt the credibility of *The Washington Times*, which had no credibility from which to subtract, being an ultra-conservative rag founded and owned by the Reverend Sun Myung Moon. Incidentally, or rather, not incidentally at all, the Reverend Sun Myung Moon is also an advocate of Intelligent Design. And I, for one, would really like to seem him take a more vocal role in the defense of said pseudo-theory. I think he would make a fantastic spokesperson for the Discovery Institute, for instance.

In the same article, Santorum also claimed that Intelligent Design is a "legitimate scientific theory that should be taught in science classes." On the other hand, amidst the immediate aftermath of Hurricane Katrina, Santorum also said the following about those who failed to leave New Orleans before the storm: "I mean people who don't heed those warnings and then put people at risk as a result of not heeding those warnings... There may be a need to look at tougher penalties on those who decide to ride it out and understand that there are consequences to not leaving." You would think drowning in fetid water and being criticized by an idiot on national television would be a suitably tough penalty, but apparently not. If only they'd had dinosaurs and high-speed circular saws like Noah did, they could have built an Ark.

* * *

Life is mysterious. The universe is mysterious. The political landscape is even more mysterious still. But if humanity has learned anything during the course of its own mysterious history – and that's a big if – it's that mysteries have a tendency to get solved, particularly if humanity really wishes to solve them.

The philosophical battle between methodological naturalism and haphazard mysticism is often amusing, occasionally hilarious, but always serious in its real implications. Philosophy has consequences. The outlook of a civilization is the nervous system of a civilization. A civilization that plucks out its own eyes because it is afraid of what it may see will stagnate, degenerate, or possibly die out altogether, because there will always be another civilization with a more reasonable outlook. This principle is simply an extension of natural selection. Those who aspire to truth, wherever it may lead them, are thus capable of making choices with reference to the truth. Those who do not have blinded themselves.

If the landscape is green, green bugs will live and orange bugs will die; the green bugs will exist unnoticed, and the orange bugs will quickly be devoured by birds. If the nature of the environment is knowable, those who seek to know it will stand a chance of knowing it. Those who seek to delude themselves will not. But knowledge is more than power. Truth is more than beauty. Evolution is more than a wild guess. And ignorance is more than a danger. It is, in fact, the only danger.

Oh, and there is no such thing as the Easter Bunny.

ACKNOWLEDGMENTS

Special thanks to Dr. K. John Murrow, who's fighting the good fight, as well as the folks at TalkOrigins.org, who have compiled what has to be the world's handiest compendium of biological facts, and Karen Lancaster who designs most intelligently.

Heartfelt thanks to Alan Dershowitz, Matt Taibbi, Bob Cesca, Cenk Uygur, David P. Mindell, Kenneth Weiss, Douglas H. Erwin, Douglas L. Erwin, David M. Williams, the Studio Time wild ones, the two Kens, Barb, the good people at Panda's Thumb, the American Museum of Natural History, the National Center for Science Education, the American Civil Liberties Union, the American Association for the Advancement of Science, Harvard University Dept. of Molecular and Cellular Biology, the Biological Society of Washington, Russel F. Doolittle of the Division of Biological Sciences at the University of California at San Diego, Texas A&M, The University of Texas, the National Academy of Sciences, the James Randi Educational Foundation, the Committee for Skeptical Inquiry, and the American Academy of Arts and Sciences, Attorney L. Lin Wood, Jonathan Alter, *The New York Times*, NBC News, and the *L.A. Times*.

Thanks also to former Senator Rick Santorum, Senator Tom Coburn, William Dembski, Michael Behe, Phillip Johnson, Stephen C. Meyer, and the late Emperor Constantine for making this such an easy book to write. Shine on, crazy diamonds.

And to all the folks at Cambridge House: Our awesome editor Rachel Trusheim; designers Jessica Gardner, Brittany Postler and Jon Wyble; Lue Williams, Ansley Thompson, Maggie Shippy, Amanda Lehner, and RC Caldwell.

And last, but certainly not least, God, without whom none of this would have been possible.